BLACK IN SCHOOL

BLACK IN SCHOOL

Afrocentric Reform,
Urban Youth,
& the Promise of
Hip-Hop Culture

SHAWN A. GINWRIGHT

Teachers College
Columbia University
New York and London

Published by Teachers College Press, 1234 Amsterdam Avenue, New York, NY 10027

Library of Congress Cataloging-in-Publication Data

Ginwright, Shawn A.
   Black in school : Afrocentric reform, urban youth & the promise of hip-hop culture / Shawn A. Ginwright.
     p. cm.
   Includes bibliographical references (p.) and index.
   ISBN 0-8077-4432-8 (cloth : alk. paper) — ISBN 0-8077-4431-X (pbk. : alk. paper)
   1. African Americans—Education. 2. Afrocentrism—United States. 3. African Americans—Race identity. 4. Hip-hop. I. Title.
   LC2717.G56 2004
   373.1829'96073—dc22   2003067213

ISBN 0-8077-4431-X (paper)
ISBN 0-8077-4432-8 (cloth)

Printed on acid-free paper

Manufactured in the United States of America

11 10 09 08 07 06 05 04   8 7 6 5 4 3 2 1

Contents

Acknowledgments

MY PROFESSIONAL EXPERIENCE COMBINES EXTENSIVE WORK IN THE Oakland community through a nonprofit youth agency that I founded in 1989 and formal training from the Graduate School of Education at the University of California at Berkeley. I had the invaluable experience of working with numerous youth, parents, community workers, teachers, and school administrators about educational issues related to black youth. From 1989 until 2001 I served as the executive director of this agency and this book comes from many conversations and discussions with and observations of thousands of youth that I have worked with over the years. Their courage and strength inspire me. These young people have given me valuable life lessons that have contributed to much of my thinking. Thank you, Randa Powell, for your honesty, courage, and intelligence. I want to thank Jessie Wimberly—continue your search, brotha, and keep your eyes on the prize. Thank you, Iesha Tyler, you keep raising the bar, sistah! Jazzy Jackson, you will never know how proud I am of you; you are the reason that I continue to do this work. I would like to acknowledge, Ronnell Clayton, your wisdom, insight, and vision for your life and your community redefines commitment. J. Braggs, Maya Locket, Kalilah Moon, thanks for not revoking my "ghetto pass." For every youth who has ever attended Camp Akili, I continue to grow and learn from your search for higher ground. Thank you for allowing me to watch and lead you through your journey. I would like to dedicate this book to Steven Avila who was an inspiration to us all; we miss you, brotha!

I would like to acknowledge the following people for their support and guidance throughout this project. Pedro Noguera, thanks for supporting my work and providing me with contacts and endless feedback and suggestions on the various drafts of this document; your continued professional guidance and friendship has been invaluable. Thank you, John Hurst and Raka Ray, for your particular expertise in social movements and liberatory practices. Julio Cammarota, thanks for listening, asking me tough questions, and making me continue even when I felt like giving up; your friendship is priceless. Inca Mohamed, your insight about youth issues and your confidence and support of my work with Leadership Excellence has kept my vision alive. To the entire West Oakland Community School crew—Lisa Stulberg, Marjorie Wilkes, Sean Irving, Macheo Payne, Anthony Reese, Akiyu Hatano, Jumoke and Greg Hodge, Jackie Buist, Marcus and AyoDeji Green—thanks for your emotional and intellectual support! I would also like to thank my colleagues at Santa Clara University—Marilyn Fernandez, Francisco Jimenez, Ramon Chacon, Alma Garcia, Steve Fugita, and Charles Powers—for your support and providing me this time to finish. John Ratliff and David Hawkins, thanks for our numerous conversations about what really matters in life.

Lastly, Mom and Dad, your strength and inspiration have given me a vision of new possibilities for our world and your love and gentle guidance are my foundation. This is also dedicated to both of my loving aunts, Auntie and Momma Joyce; thanks for your unconditional love, support, and years of unselfish giving. To both of my brothers, who I know will never read any of these words, I love you both. To Dr. Henry Wilson Jr., my "Uncle Hank," who continues to encourage educational excellence in our family. To my best friend, my love, my angel, and my wife—Nedra, you are all of these and more; without you none of these words would be possible. Your countless sacrifice, love, patience, and support continue to fill my life with meaning. I dedicated each word to my children, Takai and Nyah, who one day I hope will read this and discuss these ideas with me. Through God, all things are possible.

Introduction

MY WORK WITH AFRICAN AMERICAN CHILDREN AND YOUTH BEGAN in 1985 as a summer camp counselor for a multicultural summer leadership program for teens in Southern California. In 1989 I founded Leadership Excellence, Inc., an organization dedicated to training African American youth to address problems in their schools and communities through personal and social change. My vision was to create a space where African American children and youth could heal from traumatic life challenges, think critically about social problems, and act to change their schools and communities.

I recall during one of our meetings, a young man in the program arrived late and was clearly upset over something that had happened to him. I stopped the session to allow him to share with us why he was so upset. He began telling the group of about 30 neighborhood teenagers about a party he had attended the night before our Saturday morning session. He told us that his cousin had gotten into an altercation with another young man that ended in gun violence. He had escaped the bullets that fatally killed his cousin. Still wearing the sweaty clothes from the night before, he began to explain to us how his "crew" had already made plans for retaliation. He explained, "My folks expect me to get the fool who took out my cousin. If I don't, I'm just as dead as him." Not really wanting to retaliate, he was caught between a rock and a hard place. As we continued to talk about his options, it occurred to me that he had no other place to go to discuss his dilemma. His school did not have the resources to provide him with a counselor; he rarely attended church; and he simply had no access to a professional psychologist.

Over the years, I've listened to numerous stories where black youth encountered police brutality, coped with unimaginable family violence, struggled to support their families, contended with sexual abuse, and survived rape. I've also worked closely with their schools, many of which were not equipped to help them cope with violence and abuse. Youth in urban communities face complex economic, political, and social challenges that have serious consequences for academic performance. School safety, dropout rates, substance abuse, and homicides present formidable challenges for the schools they attend and have a profound impact on how students learn (Brooks-Gunn, Ducan, Klebanov, & Sealand, 1993). More and more working-class black youth have assumed tasks that were once the responsibilities of their parents. The struggles of finding decent work, paying rent, and juggling child care have undoubtedly placed greater challenges on youth in urban communities. For these students, academic achievement is often delimited by the economic conditions of the communities in which they live.

As an advocate for African-centered approaches to educating African American children, I have come to realize that many Afrocentric discussions and debates tend to be limited to scholars, students in the academy, educators, and some practitioners. Granted, there are groups of young self-educated members of black-nationalist organizations that subscribe to an Afrocentric philosophy, but for the most part, Afrocentric ideas have been confined primarily to the black, educated middle class. I learned from years of work with poor and working-class parents and youth that the term *Afrocentric* has little or no meaning for blacks who remain on the bottom of America's economic ladder. Equality for many poor and working-class communities means higher wages, better living conditions, and safe, clean schools. The need to reconstruct their racial identity (as Afrocentrism advocates) rarely enters the conversation.

I am concerned that the black middle class has defined the plight of blacks without adequately including the voices of the poor and working class. In doing so, the issues that poor and working-class blacks define are often marginalized and given less priority in development of public and educational policy. The voices of poor and working-class blacks are being marginalized just at the time when they should be given greater priority, given the recent wave of conservative reform efforts such as welfare reform and Three Strikes, which will without doubt impact poor and working class blacks more than any other community.

This book illustrates, through a case study of McClymonds High School in Oakland, California, that multicultural reform efforts that integrate race, ethnicity, and culture in urban school reform is indeed necessary but simply insufficient, given the pervasive impact of poverty. This book, in many respects, is meant to push urban reform efforts to seriously consider the limits of focusing entirely on multicultural strategies such as Afrocentrism. My work with poor communities and with youth who struggle to find meaning in their schools has prompted me to examine how we might conceptualize urban reform in ways that affirm black youth identity while simultaneously challenge oppressive economic conditions in their communities. I contend that Afrocentric reform must be closely tied to a critical understanding of racial and economic justice. From this perspective, black youth connect the cultural utility of Afrocentric education with the day-to-day reality of urban poverty. For those who live in communities where there are few livable-wage jobs and high crime, Afrocentric education has a deeper meaning for black youth when they act to improve quality of life issues such as school safety, child care opportunities, and after-school programs.

THE EMERGENCE OF MULTICULTURAL EDUCATION

Efforts to improve the quality of urban schools have yielded few successes. School reform initiatives, particularly in urban communities, have had little impact on the schools or the lives of the students who attend them. For African American students, this effort has been particularly challenging. In the early 1970s, educators and community activists pushed for curricular strategies that better represented children of color. Multicultural education emerged as a response to the Eurocentric bias pervasive in America's urban schools. An outgrowth of the Civil Rights movement, multicultural education was viewed as a social resource that could forge greater educational opportunities and was closely tied to the struggle for jobs, economic power, and community vitality. The goal was "to gain power to define how education for children of oppressed racial groups should be conducted" (Sleeter, 1996, p. 227). In short, multiculturalism was tied to a larger struggle for economic and political equality, and public schools became one site where this struggle was carried out.

In the early 1980s, educators and community activists saw Afrocentric educational approaches as one possible solution to the disproportionate failure among African American students in urban schools (Hilliard, Payton-Stewart, & Obadele Williams, 1990; Leake, 1992; Lee, 1994). Afrocentric education can be defined as a set of principles based on East and West African philosophy that connects cultural values with classroom practices. These principles form a common framework that views African culture as a transmitter of values, beliefs, and behaviors that can ultimately translate to educational success. The fundamental Afrocentric argument is that African American students who perform poorly in school do so in part because the curricula they encounter has little relevance to their lives and culture. Afrocentric scholars argue that cultural omissions in schooling and curricula consequently erode students' cultural and self-esteem and contribute to poor academic performance. This perspective assumes that ethnic and cultural identity is inherently linked to school performance (Hale-Benson, 1986).

Unlike some forms of multiculturalism that link educational struggles to larger issues of racial and economic justice (Anyon, 1995; Apple, 1992; Sleeter & McLaren, 1995), few Afrocentric approaches explore the relationship between racial marginalization and broader issues of economic oppression. The impact of urban problems such as poverty, safety, violence, and unemployment are rarely considered in the development and implementation of Afrocentric school reform, and as a result, many Afrocentric projects simply do not connect with students' everyday lives. In order to understand the potential impact of Afrocentric reform in urban schools, reformers must also consider the economic and political realities of the communities and cities in which schools are embedded.

The limited success of Afrocentric education has led me to a series of questions regarding Afrocentric reform in poor and working-class communities: Given the bleak economic conditions in urban communities, what are the limits of multicultural reform efforts such as Afrocentrism? How does social class function in educational reform efforts within the black community? What factors contribute to the emergence of Afrocentric reform in poor urban communities? To what extent do Afrocentric ideas affirm the identities of black youth in poor urban communities?

Despite the fact that over the past decade there has been a proliferation of Afrocentric educational projects around the country (Horwitz, 1995; C. Jackson, 1991; Murrell, 1993; Perry & Fraser, 1993; Warfield, 1992), there is a dearth of information about the outcomes, challenges, and opportunities of Afrocentric reform. These questions are particularly important because Afrocentric educational reform is most commonly practiced in low-income, low-performing, urban schools. Because these schools are invariably located in poor communities, it is also important to understand the relationship between Afrocentric initiatives and the social, political, and economic contexts from which they emerge.

The purpose of this book is to understand the community forces that thwart or promote Afrocentric educational reform in urban schools located in low-income communities, and to highlight how black middle-class leaders in one urban community shaped Afrocentric education in a way that was disconnected from the experiences of working-class African American youth. As a result, the reform effort failed to transform the school because the project was not relevant to the student's day-to-day lives. This book provides important lessons about how to build multiclass coalitions in community change efforts, and key strategies about how to engage young people in school and community reform efforts. I seek to expand current Afrocentric theory and strategies by considering the impact of social class on Afrocentric education. This is accomplished in three ways. First, I argue that while Afrocentric curricula can provide an important critique of education for African American students, Afrocentric approaches in urban school reform, as they are currently implemented, are unable to address the challenges presented by urban poverty.

Second, the book provides a comprehensive story about how McClymonds High School became an Afrocentric school in 1992 and its subsequent outcomes. By focusing on how the Afrocentric project at McClymonds transpired, the book examines the economic conditions and political decisions that prompted the Oakland Unified School District (OUSD) to approve and implement an Afrocentric reform initiative at McClymonds High School. McClymonds is located in West Oakland, which is the city's poorest community. During the 1992–93 school year, 93 percent of all McClymonds students qualified for AFDC (Aid to Families with Dependent Children) and nearly 60 percent qualified for free or reduced lunch. During the same year, the 637 students who attended McClymonds comprised the lowest high school enrollments in the district. The suspension rate had soared from 10 percent during the 1992–93 school year to 24 percent during the 1995–96 school year. In 1995–96, 85 percent of McClymond's students and 80 percent of its teachers were African American. Following a nationwide movement aimed at improving education for African American students, black middle-class professionals and advocates of Afrocentric reform shaped the school reform project at McClymonds High School. I argue that members of the black middle class, in wielding considerable influence in reform of urban schools, often overlook the concerns that working class communities have about their schools.

Third, I explain how Afrocentric reform might be modified to better meet the needs of youth from low-income working-class communities. Through an analysis of successes and challenges from the Afrocentric project at McClymonds High School, I provide a more comprehensive picture about the limits and possibilities for identity-based reform in poor urban schools. Strategies that both build ethnic identity and prepare African American youth to change relevant community problems are necessary steps for future Afrocentric reform efforts.

WHAT WE DON'T KNOW ABOUT AFROCENTRIC REFORM

There are a number of things that are simply unknown about the impact of Afrocentric reform. First, how does Afrocentric reform prepare students to address issues in their lives outside the context of schools? I argue that Afrocentric strategies, in order to truly be effective, should address the ways that poor and working-class culture influences the identities of African American students in low-income urban communities.

For example, earning money through braiding hair, selling T-shirts, baby-sitting, working two part-time jobs at local fast-food restaurants all contribute to an identity of work among youth. Current Afrocentric reform efforts have focused primarily on a static view of African American youth identity by an overemphasis on West African and Egyptian philosophies that are difficult to translate, in a meaningful way, to the challenges many black youth must navigate. I argue that Afrocentric educators must consider how black youth construct complex identities that move beyond race and include issues of social class, gender, and sexuality. Youth in low-income urban communities define themselves not only by race and ethnic culture, but also by the neighborhoods in which they live, the schools they attend, gang affiliations, and certainly hip-hop culture. This book illustrates how Afrocentric reformers can develop a more complete model of African American youth identity.

Second, how do youth themselves respond to Afrocentric curriculum? This study provides insight into the ways in which African American students' lives outside of school bear on Afrocentric educational reform. My aim is to give voice to African American students' experiences in Afrocentric reform and shed light on how their identities and lives outside of school influence what happens inside of school. While empirical research regarding Afrocentric education has advocated its need and usefulness for African American students, surprisingly most researchers have all but ignored the experiences and voices of students themselves. Much of what we know about the impact of Afrocentric education is confined to a classroom-level analysis based on the experiences and perceptions of teachers. For example, Murrell (1993) examined schools in Milwaukee and highlighted the problems that emerge when white teachers instruct black students. He maintained that white teachers often do not share African American students' cultural backgrounds and as a consequence fail to provide African American students with a meaningful learning experience. Because Murrell's study focused on the classroom, we know little about how students themselves experienced Afrocentric education.

Third, how does Afrocentric education translate to higher academic performance? This book examines some outcome measures such as grade point averages, school suspension, attendance, and graduation rates and offers conclusions about the effectiveness of this particular Afrocentric initiative. Few studies have examined the academic outcomes derived from Afrocentric education. This is largely because many Afrocentric reform initiatives are relatively new and there is hesitancy on the part of researchers to make premature conclusions about this highly politicized reform initiative. As the book will demonstrate, empirical research bears the risk of exposing shortcomings of particular Afrocentric initiatives, which then becomes fuel for the entrenched opposition to Afrocentrism.

OVERVIEW OF THE BOOK

This book is composed of eight chapters that will provide a comprehensive story about the Afrocentric transformation of McClymonds High School in 1992 and its subsequent outcomes. Chapter 1 traces the historical development of the Afrocentric movement and highlights the specific ways in which Afrocentrism becomes a movement of the black middle class. In this chapter, I illustrate how the black middle class has transformed Black Nationalism of the late 1960s into an intellectual movement that aims to reclaim, reconstruct, and reposition black identity. Chapter 1 also explores forces responsible for the emergence of Afrocentric education. Chapter 2 locates Afrocentric reform in the broader terrain of urban education and provides background on Afrocentrism and how it is used in urban schools. Rather than conceptualizing urban school reform as if it were somehow separate from the community in which it occurs, I argue that the problems confronting urban schools are a result of social and economic patterns that support deeply rooted racist practices in poor urban communities.

Building from Chapter 2, Chapter 3 looks more closely at Oakland and examines the historical and contemporary forces that have come to shape the city's economy and politics. Specifically, it outlines the growth of Oakland's black middle class and reveals the forces responsible for the emergence of Oakland's urban poor. Chapter 4 narrows the lens of analysis and focuses on Oakland Unified School District. From the perspective of working-class community residents, Chapter 4 provides a vivid look at the West Oakland community and describes the everyday struggles and victories of finding affordable housing and employment and maintaining kinship support. From the perspective of parents, teachers, and students, this chapter also describes the everyday reality of McClymonds High.

Chapter 5 examines the Afrocentric reform initiative at McClymonds High School and demonstrates the different ways in which community residents, professional educational consultants, teachers, and school administrators involved with the project diagnosed the problems at the school. Chapter 6 looks more closely at the process of implementing the project at the school and explores the tensions, barriers, and challenges the project confronted. Chapter 7 offers a discussion about the outcomes of the Afrocentric initiative and explains why the project failed to improve the school.

Chapter 8 offers an alternative Afrocentric model for the hip-hop generation. For children and youth who have grown up in urban communities in the post–civil rights era where good-paying jobs are scarce, violence is commonplace, and families are unstable, urban educational reform must take into account how black youth navigate their lives inside and outside of school environments.

From October 1997 to September 1998, I had numerous conversations and conducted formal and informal interviews with community residents, teachers, school administrators, and high school students. This story is also a synthesis of evidence from materials such as school performance reports, newsletters, unpublished manuscripts, memoranda, curricula, training manuals, community flyers, newsletters, and official school documents. This case study is also ethnographic because Oakland is my home. In 1994 my wife and I moved to Oakland, and a year later we purchased a home in a mixed-income neighborhood in East Oakland. Since I moved to Oakland, I have been deeply involved with educational and youth-related issues in the community. While in graduate school, I continued to work as the executive director of Leadership Excellence and developed relationships with community residents, Oakland Unified School District officials, and school administrators and youth in several local high schools. My role, as both a researcher and an educator, was helpful in developing relationships with community members because I had already worked with them in other capacities. In qualitative research, I would be certainly considered an insider. By living and working in Oakland, I had the distinct advantage of knowing "the lay of the land." Consequently, I experienced few problems getting around and was well aware of the major changes occurring in Oakland. For example, in West Oakland, my primary site, I witnessed over a period of 3 years the removal of thousands of units of federally subsidized housing, and I have become acquainted with some of the displaced residents of this redevelopment. Some of this case study borrows from these informal conversations that I have had with residents of West Oakland and from acquaintances who work in the West Oakland community.

ONE

Say It Loud, I'm Black and I'm Proud! Afrocentric Movement, Past, Present, and Future

THERE ARE A NUMBER OF MOMENTS IN THE HISTORY OF BLACK America when nationalist ideas become ripe. If conceptualized as a form of Black Nationalism, the concept of Afrocentrism can be traced as far back as 1750. In this view, Afrocentrism can be understood as a set of principles that aims to liberate blacks through reeducation; establishing economic, political, and religious self-sufficiency; and creating a nation through land acquisition. Paul Cuffe, a free-born eighteenth-century philanthropist, merchant, sea captain, and son of a former slave may be credited with the first Black Nationalist movement in 1815 with his voyage to Sierra Leone with former slaves. In 1852 Martin Delany—another early Black Nationalist and abolitionist—argued that black people were in fact a nation similar to various stateless minority groups within the nations of Europe and that, as a national group, blacks should seek a territory (Carlise, 1975). In 1873 Alexander Crummell—an ordained priest, scholar, and early Black Nationalist—urged blacks in the United States to return with him to Liberia to establish a black Christian republic. Carlise noted that Crummell's ideas influenced W. E. B. DuBois, who in turn had a profound impact on both African and American nationalists' ideas. DuBois played a significant role in the intellectual progress of the movement by advocating cultural pride and economic and political development for Africans throughout the world. It wasn't until 1914 when Marcus Garvey formed the Universal Negro Improvement Conservation Association (UNIA) that the movement took hold in black America. Migrating from Jamaica, Garvey became well aware of the conditions facing black Americans and was enormously successful in mobilizing thousands of blacks around the nationalist ideology. Influenced by his predecessors (Crummell, DuBois, and Booker T. Washington), Garvey advocated black-owned business, the end of white rule in Africa, and the reclamation of land in Africa. His Back to Africa plan followed the tradition of Crummell, and although it was a failed attempt, it highlights the mass base and influence Garveyism had on Black Nationalist thought.

Harold Cruse (1967) noted that Garvey played such a significant role in the formation of Black Nationalist ideas, that virtually every movement in black America since has its roots in Garveyism. Similarly, Carlise (1975) suggested that many movements, such as the rise of the Nation of Islam, drew leadership from ex-Garveyites and highlighted the fact that Elijah Poole, who later became Elijah Mohammed ("Prophet" in the Nation of Islam), was a "corporal" in the UNIA Chicago chapter. Furthermore, he noted that "the greatest growth of the later movements was in the same cities and among the same social groups as the core of the Garvey movement" (p. 129).

The black church also played a significant role in the propagation of Black Nationalism. As Carlise noted, "From its beginnings in the late eighteenth century, the black church in the United States had incorporated several principles of separatism. . . . By their nature as separately organized, separately managed, and separately financed enterprises, the black churches were crucial to the evolution of Black Nationalist ideas" (p. 131). Although non-Christian, the most notable is perhaps the Nation of Islam. In 1933 the first temple was established under the leadership of the newly appointed minister Elijah Mohammed. Addressing the everyday needs of suffering blacks by infusing Black Nationalist themes into sermons, the Nation of Islam was successful in attracting thousands into its membership. In 1954 Malcolm X was appointed minister of the New York temple and gained international popularity through his passionate, eloquent, and poignant oratory. Malcolm, like his predecessors (Crummell, Delany, Garvey), called for black self-determination through economics and education and transformation of negative notions of blackness to positive views of black identity. It wasn't long before slogans like "black is beautiful" and "say it loud, I'm black and I'm proud" became commonplace for blacks. Black college students and unemployed urban blacks who were discontented with the ineffectiveness of the nonviolent protest typical of the Civil Rights movement, called for a more radical ideology of Black Power.

URBAN PROTEST AND THE BLACK POWER MOVEMENT

From 1966 to 1967 the rhetoric of Black Power spawned a rise in both cultural and political consciousness for blacks. Posey (1969) noted that black protest organizations up until 1966 were operating without an ideology that could win the trust and confidence of alienated and impoverished blacks. The rise of Black Power, he claimed, "heightened the 'consciousness' of the black masses to such an extent that the disintegrating black protest organizations experienced a rebirth of purpose" (p. 254). Articulated by Stokely Carmichael, Black Power was a movement for and about the black masses. Marable (1984) argued that Black Power was embraced by the black community and widely integrated into various areas of black life. He stated that "black people were addressing each other as 'brother' when they passed in the streets; 'soul food' restaurants became a matter of community pride; 'black history' the all-consuming topic; Malcolm X the authoritative source. Even seven-year-old black children seemed to know a phrase or two of Swahili" (p. 110). The concept of Black Power became even more popular among the masses as its ideology became more integrated into the everyday lives of urban blacks.

Black Power ideology came to mean three fundamental things: cultural, economic, and political liberation. The concept rested on the premise that before a group could enter the open society, it must establish power through solidarity and sovereignty (Carmichael & Hamilton, 1969). With Black Nationalist overtones, Black Power's first guiding principle was solidarity among black people. Also rooted in the ideology of Black Power was the notion that an African worldview and African principles should be placed at the center of black consciousness. Embracing Black Power would mean rejecting European culture and reclaiming Africa as a basis for a reconstituted racial identity. For example, Carmichael and Hamilton argued, "The extent to which black Americans can and do 'trace their roots' to Africa, to that extent will they be able to be more effective on the political scene" (p. 245). In this context, the cultural is the political. The combination of Pan-Africanism and Black Nationalism provided Black Power with both a cultural and political agenda that placed Africa at the center of both political and cultural discussions.

The Black Power movement urged black Americans to come together not merely as an oppressed class, but more important as a racial and cultural group. Carson (1981) noted that the movement "emphasized race rather than class and Third World alliances rather than coalitions with poor whites" (p. 227). Racial identity and political and economic solidarity became the framework for the Black Power movement.

The movement, however, underwent a significant shift in 1967. Up until 1966, the Civil Rights movement had placed a premium on direct action and practical forms of mobilizing. As Cruse (1967) has pointed out, the Black Power movement became, by contrast, more rhetorical than revolutionary. Black Power had transformed from direct action for tactics to achieve desegregation toward ideology and theories about the black condition. It is within this ideological shift of rejecting European ideology and embracing Africanness that we find the roots of contemporary Afrocentrism.

As the Black Nationalist movement became more entrenched in black America, like other forms of black cultural expressions, Black Power was ultimately seized by and co-opted into the American mainstream. In 1967 a black Republican, Nathan Wright, organized the first major Black Power conference. Marable (1984) noted that the conference was held in a plush, white-owned hotel and the high registration fee restricted the number of black working-class and activist attendees. The second conference, in 1968, was cosponsored by a white corporation: Clairol Company. In short, Marable argued that Black Power became synonymous with black capitalism.

FROM THE STREETS TO THE IVORY TOWERS

Black Power ultimately had a profound effect on two institutions in American society: (1) electoral politics such as voting and electing government representatives and (2) institutional representation in large companies and universities. Posey (1969) argued that "nothing is more evident of the impact the 'Black Power' concept has had than is the emergence of black student unions on college campuses, black student associations, black social work associations, black business associations, and black political parties" (p. 257). Politically, Black Power exercised voting power by electing black officials at an unprecedented rate. By 1969 there were over 1,000 black elected officials across the country. By 1975 that number nearly tripled to 3,000 black elected officials (Marable, 1984). Marable, however, argued that many of these newly elected officials were middle class and relied on the black middle-class vote. The Black Power movement also forged its way into America's predominantly white institutions, opening the doors for a new black middle class. In corporate America, blacks in professional, managerial and administrative positions increased 57 percent from 1973 to 1982. In colleges and universities, the number of blacks enrolled full time nearly doubled between 1970 and 1980 (W. J. Wilson, 1987).

In 1968, the first black studies department was established at San Francisco State University under the leadership of Nathan Hare. The department came about through virulent battles between students and administrators (McEvoy & Miller, 1969). These battles, however, were not confined to San Francisco State University; in fact, McEvoy and Miller documented similar battles at Duke, Columbia, and the University of California at Berkeley. Karenga (1989) noted that many of these battles were waged by Black Power advocates. The struggle for black studies existed in a larger context of black liberation and was fueled by both radical Black Power groups such as the Student Nonviolent Coordinating Committee (SNCC) and more conservative Black Power advocates among faculty already in universities. Baker (1993) noted that as early as 1973 the United States had over 200 black studies programs, most with all-black faculty.

By 1974 black studies faced a dual tension—one from within the university community and the other from within black intellectual communities. The first tension came from academic critics who claimed that black studies lacked academic integrity and created racial separatism (Wilkins, 1969). This was due in part to the emphasis black studies programs placed on community activism and service activities (Hine, 1992). Nevertheless, black studies challenged the traditional structure of academe by bridging the campus and the community and calling for more practical and meaningful instruction. For example, Hare (1969) argued that "a black studies program which is not revolutionary and nationalistic is, accordingly, quite profoundly irrelevant" (p. 234). Karenga (1989) noted that "the Black Student movement stressed the need to bring the campus to the community and the community to the campus" (p. 134).

The influence of the Black Power movement was also felt in professional associations that studied the African continent. In 1969 black members of the U.S. African Studies Association (ASA) split from the group after realizing that the mostly white organization would not take a more critical approach toward studying African people; the formation of the new African Heritage Studies Association allowed black academics to study Africa from a point of view that encompassed native perspectives. At the 1969 ASA conference, the newly formed black caucus of the association, led by John Henrik Clarke of Hunter College in New York, demanded that the African Studies Association make sweeping changes in its purpose. After the black caucus closed down the conference through orchestrated protest and disruptions, B. D. Bargar presented the following statement:

> African peoples attending the ASA conference have demanded that the study of African life be undertaken from a Pan-Africanist perspective. This perspective defines that all black people are African peoples and negates the tribalization of African peoples. . . . African peoples will no longer permit our people to be raped culturally, economically, politically, and intellectually merely to provide European scholars with intellectual status symbols of African artifacts hanging in their living rooms and irrelevant and injurious lectures for their classrooms. (quoted by Howe, 1998, p. 62)

The second tension black studies experienced was the ongoing polemic between two nationalist traditions found in the black activist community.

In one camp were the cultural nationalists, who defined the crisis in black life in cultural terms. For cultural nationalists, a black cultural revolution was needed to "break the monopoly the oppressor has on black minds and begin to rescue and reconstruct black history and humanity in their own image and interests" (Karenga, 1989, p. 133). Advocates of this position included Maulana Karenga, Amiri Baraka, and Haki Madhubuti. In the other camp were the revolutionary nationalists, who subscribed to Marxist-based views of the black condition. Here activists sought to challenge capitalism and infuse socialism into the American polity by redistributing wealth and establishing a separate "black nation." In this view, black liberation would come only through the establishment and ownership of black economies, institutions, and communities. For them, class suffering framed their analysis of the black condition. Ultimately, both forms of nationalism fueled tensions between social reformation (indicative of the cultural nationalists) on the one hand, and social revolution (indicative of the revolutionary nationalists) on the other.

During the late 1960s both cultural and revolutionary orientations vied for influence on black studies departments (Hall, 1991; Hine, 1992). In addition, black studies scholars, some of whom were black activists, ushered this debate into the university (Kershaw, 1992). For example, Maulana Karenga, the founder of the cultural nationalist organization United Slaves, brought to California State University at Los Angeles not only a more radical social theory, but also a cultural nationalist perspective for understanding black life. In 1968 at the University of California at Los Angeles, Arthur Smith (who later changed his name to Molefi Asante) demonstrated the influence of the nationalist debate in his early writings. A member of the Department of Speech Communication, Smith (1969) pointed to particular rhetorical devices used in what he called the "Black Revolution." Throughout his analysis, he cited sources such as Malcolm X, Maulana Karenga, Stokely Carmichael, and other Black Nationalist advocates.

Both cultural nationalist and revolutionary nationalists played their part in shaping black studies departments throughout the country. From within the university, black scholars were forced to search for ways to "legitimize" black studies through recognized and respected academic canons such as anthropology, sociology, and political science; at the same time they sought to challenge traditional Western orientations to knowledge. Attempting to resolve these tensions from both inside and outside the university, black studies found itself in a precarious position. In order to survive, black studies needed to establish academic legitimacy while maintaining its philosophical commitment to activism.

Conservative Climate

The conservative 20-year span from 1970 to 1990 transformed black life in general and black studies in particular. The gains that had been made from the Civil Rights movement and the Black Power movement came under attack. By the late 1970s, conservative critics began to react to the liberal reforms particularly found in education. These critics argued that liberal reforms for educational opportunities had resulted in a decline in educational standards. Allan Bloom's (1987) work is indicative of this conservative climate. Bloom argued that the university had experienced an intellectual decline and lack of purpose that had been brought on by a cultural void in American society. Karenga (1989) noted that the rise of the right wing advocated Christian fundamentalism, Reaganomics, and a host of political and social rearrangements that undercut the advances gained during the 1960s.

During this period the rising tide of conservatism removed educational opportunities for blacks and threatened the vitality of black studies departments. Ronald Reagan's presidential victory was translated to (1) a financial cut in educational programs, (2) a diminishing role by the government to provide social and economic equality, and (3) attacks on affirmative action (Cookson, Sadovnik, & Semel, 1992). While black studies had always been under attack by conservatives from both inside and outside the ivory towers of academe (Baker, 1993; Ford, 1973; Hine, 1992), black studies scholars transformed the cultural nationalist tradition into an formal academic area of study called African American or Africana studies. The rise in identity movements during the 1980s coupled with the promotion of a procapitalist agenda by black leaders prompted black scholars, activists, and intellectuals to abandon Marxist orientations to the study of black life altogether (Marable, 1996; Rivers, 1992). As a result, cultural nationalist ideas gained popularity among black scholars and became a more viable strategy to critique forms of Western domination.

Turning to Cheikh Anta Diop and other African writers, scholars such as Molefi Asante, Maulana Karenga, Oba T'Shaka, Nathan Hare, and Wade Nobles formalized the Black Nationalist tradition into a theoretical framework called *Afrocentrism*, which is a worldview and theoretical perspective that is based in East and West African philosophy. Initially the movement began from scholarship within certain black studies departments. Integrating theoretical material from African scholars and borrowing heavily from the Black Nationalist tradition, in 1980 Molefi Asante transformed the Afrocentric framework into a formal theory. Black college students at institutions like Temple University and San Francisco State

University were introduced to Afrocentric theory and integrated it into their respective disciplines and lifestyles.

THE AFROCENTRIC MOVEMENT TODAY

Afrocentrism emerged as a result of at least two factors. First, the momentum of Black Power created both the structural opportunities and the ideological climate for establishment of black studies departments. Black studies served as a "safe haven," which attempted to be a bridge between the black community and the university. This attempt challenged the traditional ivory tower position of the university and created tension between the university and black studies departments. Second, the conservative attack on educational and economic opportunities during the 1970s and 1980s resulted in a rising interest in expanding black ownership of business and developing black entrepreneurs that dominated the intellectual and social landscape. As cultural nationalism and revolutionary nationalism vied for influence on the scope and direction of black studies departments, scholars abandoned Marixism as a viable theoretical framework to study black life. Taken together, Afrocentrism emerged as a need to (1) legitimize black studies departments and (2) resolve the cultural vs. revolutionary nationalist debate by formalizing cultural nationalist orientations.

The emergence of Afrocentrism became an effective framework to accomplish these ends. By 1990 Afrocentrism had transcended its ivory tower birth and become a social movement in black life. In communities throughout the United States, black bookstores, Kenté cloth, and African masks became icons of the movement's influence on black identity. Although black studies departments generally have declined since the 1970s, some, such as the African American Studies Department at Temple University, have gained prominence. In addition, Afrocentrism's effort to resolve the cultural vs. revolutionary nationalist debate has not been realized. In fact, these two camps are evident among many contemporary Afrocentric scholars today (Marable, 1993). Nevertheless, Afrocentrism has created a new terrain for this old debate.

Afrocentrism has taken on a new meaning since the early 1980s. For example, since 1985 nearly 300 "Afrocentric" schools have sprung up throughout the country ("African Dreams," 1991; Toch, 1991; "The Year of the Black Author," 1995). Since the early 1980s, there has been a growing demand by black educators to implement Afrocentric curricula in both public and private schools (Karp, 1991). Since 1985 there has been a growing market for books written by and about African Americans. Responding to this demand, from 1985 to 1994 black America experienced an explosion of Afrocentric books and bookstores that specialized in Afro-centric materials. In 1993 alone African Americans spent approximately $178 million dollars on Afrocentric books ("The year," 1995). If one were to visit virtually any street fair or community festival in black America, inevitably one would find numerous African icons such as Kenté cloth and African clothing.

WHAT IS AFROCENTRISM?

Afrocentrism has been described as a set of principles that place Africa at the center of political, economic, cultural, and spiritual life for African Americans. At its most fundamental level, Afrocentrism challenges the claim that all modern knowledge resides in the Western world (Asante, 1987). Proponents of the Afrocentric movement assert that the hegemonic forces that emanate from a European-centered or a Eurocentric paradigm are ill equipped to understand the African American experience. They argue that Afrocentricity rejects a Eurocentric worldview and "adopts Africa as a takeoff point in any discussion of African civilization" (Oyebade, 1990). In short, Afrocentrism is an ideological perspective that places Africa at the center of African American identity.

Afrocentrism is also a worldview that not only transforms the ways in which blacks understand themselves in relation to white America, but also challenges predominantly white institutions to acknowledge the ex-clusion of African American identity. This form of cultural nationalism is not a new phenomenon for African Americans. Marcus Garvey's Back to Africa movement, Carter G. Woodson's writings that emphasize the need for black Americans to embrace an African identity, and the Black Power movement during the 1960s all suggest that there are certain moments in African American history when people are compelled to reconstruct and give new meaning to their collective identities.

The Afrocentric movement is not without exception. Afrocentric pro-ponents agree that many African Americans, particularly children and youth, suffer from an ethnic identity crisis and that rediscovering West African and Egyptian philosophies holds the promise of cultural transfor-mation for blacks. Building ethnic pride, strengthening knowledge about African history, and fostering a worldview that values community, bal-ance, and harmony is one promising strategy to improve the quality of life for blacks. Despite the movement's popularity among educators, how-ever, the Afrocentric explosion has been largely confined to intellectual debates within academia. Through black studies departments, Afrocentric ideas have been used to address many issues in the black community, particularly in education. However, most of the writing about Afrocentrism has been limited to two opposing views within academia (Wilkenson, 1996; J. A. Wilson, 1994).

Afrocentric Proponents

Discussions about Afrocentrism generally fall into one of two categories— proponents of Afrocentrism or opponents of Afrocentrism. Proponents of Afrocentrism typically argue for the need, validity, and usefulness of Afrocentric theories. There are three basic types of Afrocentric proponents: classical, critical, and nationalist.

Classical Afrocentric theories are concerned with rejecting notions of cultural inferiority and promoting the idea that Africa, particularly Egypt, played a major role in the direction and shape of Western civilization (Ben-Jochannon, 1972; Bernal, 1987). The central theme in classical Afrocentric research is that Africa, in general, and Egypt, in particular, provided the origin of civilization. Such discussions often refer to Egypt as being the foundation and progenitor of the world's science, philosophy, and religion (Akbar, 1984; Bernal, 1987; Diop, 1974). Afrocentric scholars reclaim Africa as the mother of civilization and reject Western interpretations of history, which only highlight and glorify Europe.

Much of the foundation for classical Afrocentric research emanates from the work of Cheikh Anta Diop. In his groundbreaking research, *The African Origin of Civilization* (1974), Diop argued that historical, archeological, and anthropological evidence support the theory that ancient Egypt and its citizens were Negroid in origin: "In contemporary descriptions of the ancient Egyptians, this question is never raised. Eyewitnesses of that period formally affirm that the Egyptians were Blacks" (p. 1). Diop's well-documented research has served as the bedrock for both rejecting European cultural supremacy and reestablishing Africa as the origin of civilization in classical Afrocentric research.

Borrowing from the work of Diop, Martin Bernal challenged the accepted belief that ancient Egyptians were Caucasian (Bernal, 1987). In *Black Athena, the Afroasiatic Roots of Classical Civilization*, Bernal also rejected the notion that Africans were inferior to Europeans. His central argument was that much of classical Western civilization has its roots in North African societies. Numerous historians, Egyptologists, and anthropologists have used both Diop and Bernal as the foundation of their research (Browder, 1992; Hilliard, 1978; Jackson, 1939).

What has proved to be most useful from the classical strategy is its ability to provide alternative narratives, histories, and viewpoints from European claims to Western civilization. For African American children and youth, this approach can provide a powerful way to connect to lessons in areas where African Americans have traditionally been excluded. However, while the classical strategy may encourage cultural esteem, it presents a static view of race and culture and avoids a class analysis that might highlight the economic and political power differences within the African American community (Akinyela, 1995; Haymes, 1995b; Lemelle, 1993; Marable, 1993; McCarthy, 1995).

The second type of Afrocentric proponent could be categorized as critical Afrocentrism, which was introduced by Akinyela (1990) as a philosophy concerned with liberating African people from multiple forms of domination. By exploring strategies that address human suffering brought on by multiple forms of oppression such as racism, sexism and poverty, critical Afrocentrism focuses on liberationist practices for humanity (Akinyela, 1990; Asante, 1980). Critical Afrocentric scholars and educators concentrate on the various ways in which African-centered ideology can critically inform the everyday lives of Africans throughout the diaspora. It calls attention to culture as a formative process and accommodates the complex interaction of race, class, gender, and sexuality.

Most critical Afrocentric scholarship concentrates on the various ways in which African-centered ideology can provide a lens to view and understand African's lives around the world. Central to critical Afrocentric scholarship is the notion that due to Western ontology, classical philosophy and theories are unable to effectively critique the African American experience. Criticalists argue that a Western worldview is based on rationality, linear time, individualism, and control, all of which run counter to an African worldview, which views time as cyclical and values community and collective participation (Asante, 1996; Harris, 1992). Consequently, a more appropriate *ontology* (view of the world) and *epistemology* (verifications of those views) is one that centers the African experience in an African worldview (Kershaw, 1992). The way in which critical Afrocentrists view Western and African ontology is represented in Table 1.1 adapted from Linda Myers (1988).

One example of how African-centered ideology can critically inform the everyday lives of Africans throughout the diaspora is provided in the work of Molife Asante. In 1980, borrowing from the prior work of Diop, Asante (1980) published *Afrocentricity: Theory of Social Change*. Through what he refers to as an "African Cultural System," Asante argued that Afrocentricity "questions the approach you make to reading, writing, jogging, running, eating, keeping healthy, seeing, studying, loving, struggling, and working" (p. 45). In short, Afrocentrism, according to Asante, is a framework or worldview that allows one to critique the Western world while functioning more effectively within it.

Table 1.1. Opposing World Views

Afrocentric World View	*Western World View*
Self-knowledge is the basis of all knowledge. All is symbolic of spirit and manifesting.	*External-knowledge* is the basis of all knowledge. One knows through counting and measuring.
Both/And mode of reasoning.	*Either/Or* mode of reasoning.
Spirituality is the process by which goals will be achieved.	*Technology* is the most valued process by which goals will be reached.
Faith, choice, consciousness, belief are primary.	*Control* is the primary goal.
Choosing, acting, and creating define power.	*Money, influence, and politics* define power.
Happiness and peace define the purpose of life.	*Owning and possessing* define life's purpose.
Loves change and growth.	*Fears* change and internal growth.

Adapted from L. J. Myers, 1988.

Borrowing from Asante and others, critical Afrocentric scholars have applied an Afrocentric philosophy to their respective disciplines: in psychology (Akbar, 1991; Jones, 1991; Karenga, 1989; Meyers, 1988), communication (Asante, 1983), and education (Dei, 1994; Detroit Public Schools, 1992; Hilliard et al., 1990; Murtadha, 1995; Perry & Fraser, 1993; Shujaa, 1994). However, while critical Afrocentrism provides us with the most comprehensive models for understanding the complexities of the African American experience, it does not dominate Afrocentric theory and practices (Akinyela, 1990; Asante, 1980).

The third type of Afrocentric proponent is the nationalist. Nationalists are those who borrow from the historical legacy of Black Nationalism and integrate nationalist themes into both theory and practice. This type of Afrocentrism is perhaps most closely related to its predecessor—the Black Nationalist movement. Nationalists often advocate for economic, political, and spiritual self-determination, and seek ways to unify the experiences of blacks around the world (Henderson, 1995). Rejecting integration as a means to bring about racial equality, nationalist Afrocentrists seek "nationhood" or unification by promoting ways for African Americans to own, control, and operate their own institutions. Scholars and practitioners advocate developing banks, businesses, and schools. For example, Shujaa (1994) argued that African Americans should begin to create and control their own schools:

> It clearly makes no sense to expect a system of schooling controlled by the
> politically dominant culture for its own interests to provide education for
> African Americans. . . . In many cities, African-centered independent schools
> are providing a means for acquiring educational control. (p. 32)

Shujaa advocated that African Americans control their own educational institutions in order to transmit African cultural knowledge. What is important for nationalists is that African Americans control institutions as well as the practices within. Therefore, while many nationalists may advocate for the use of Afrocentric pedagogies, curricula, and materials in public schools, they would still argue that such approaches are insufficient because public schools are not controlled by blacks for blacks.

Another group of nationalist proponents includes those who promote cultural uplift and development for diasporic Africans. These scholars and practitioners are concerned with nation building through shared African culture. Perhaps the best-known advocate for cultural nationalism is Maulana Karenga. Karenga was the leader of the Back to Black cultural movement during the 1960s and was known as one of the primary leaders of the cultural nationalist movement. He is the creator of *Kawadia*, the theory of cultural and social change that includes the festival *Kwanzaa*, which is now celebrated by people of African descent all over the world.

While nationalist Afrocentrism does provide a class-based critique of the black condition, it is often embedded within religious beliefs that rarely link the struggles of African American poor to broader issues of gender and sexual oppression. Additionally, despite the fact that some disenfranchised black youth have adopted a nationalist critique of American society through hip-hop culture (Kelley, 1996), nationalist Afrocentric educators have been unable to make the connection between the suffering of black youth and the need for liberationist practices in the classroom (Haymes, 1995a; Marable, 1992).

All types of Afrocentric proponents confront the overtly racist representations of Africa in Western versions of world history while celebrating an African worldview. Their focus on the true racial origins of Western civilization is central to challenging European domination of Western culture. The challenge that Afrocentrism poses, however, is not without a response. Scholars opposing Afrocentric ideas have provided a healthy and heated debate about the validity of an Afrocentric worldview.

Afrocentric Opponents

Opponents of Afrocentrism generally point out its inaccuracy, cultural chauvinism, and political futility for African Americans. Similar to Afrocentric proponents, there are strands within the oppositional literature. In the first strand the Euro-originists attempt to invalidate and discredit proponents of Egyptian contributions to the world (Lefkowitz, 1993, 1996; Ravitch, 1990).These scholars attempt to defend the traditional study of ancient civilization by arguing that the contributions of Greece and Rome are the canons of Western civilization. The primary point of contention is whether or not ancient Greece is the cornerstone of the Western world. Scholars from this camp argue that Afrocentrism mythologizes and romanticizes ancient Egypt (Early, 1995; Lemelle, 1993) and refer to historical documents and text in order to find inaccuracies and fallacies in the Afrocentric argument.

Mary Lefkowitz in *Not Out of Africa* (1996) maintains that much Afrocentric literature and research contradicts the evidence of well-known historical and anthropological scholarship. She vehemently rejects the notion that ancient Egyptians were black. She bases her premise on the fact that Egyptians themselves never considered themselves black Africans and consciously disassociated themselves from black Africans:

> The native population of the North [Africa] was the ancestors of the modern Berbers: they are shown in Egyptian art with light hair and facial coloring. . . . For that reason, it is unlikely that most natives of what was called "Africa" in antiquity, that is North Africa, were "black" in the modern sense of the word. (p. 31)

In many ways, Euro-originists are responding to the claims made by originists such as Cheikh Anta Diop and Yosef A. Ben-Jᴏchannon, who maintain that Egyptians were black. Euro-originists aim to reject notions of race-based origins while at the same time debunking the "myths" of African origins of civilization (Lefkowitz, 1993, 1996).

A second strand within the oppositional camp can be described as a Neomarxist critique of Afrocentrism. Neomarxists argue that Afrocentrism fails to problematize social class and lacks political praxis (Early, 1995; Lemelle, 1993; Marable & Lullings, 1994). Reviving a perennial debate among black intellectuals, which has its roots in Black Nationalism (Cruse, 1967), these scholars argue that Afrocentrism overlooks the overwhelming influence of social class and economic exigencies on the lives of poor and working-class African Americans. The Neomarxist critique maintains that Afrocentric scholarship lacks an analysis of capitalism and the consequent owner-worker relationship. Neomarxists claim that African Americans' experiences can be examined more appropriately by understanding the relationship between means of work and owners of production (Lemelle, 1993).

Neomarxist scholars have also attacked Afrocentrism for "essentializing" the concept of race (Marable, 1993). They argue that Afrocentric proponents have a tendency to homogenize the multivaried and complex histories and experiences of people of African descent. For example, Lemelle (1993) argued that

> Anyone who has studied African history and its people and cultures seriously realizes that a multitude of attitudes and cosmologies brought about its many cultures—none of which were "universal". Africa is made up of people from different ethnic, religious, and linguistic groupings. (p. 97)

Similarly, others have argued that Afrocentrism has been applied to African Americans as if they were a monolithic group and tends to treat race as a static phenomenon (McCarthy, 1995). The contempt and ferociousness involved in this debate was clear in Marable's (1993) statement:

> Vulgar Afrocentrists deliberately ignored or obscured the historical reality of social class stratification within the African Diaspora. They essentially argued that the interests of all black people—from Joint Chiefs of Staff Chairman General Colin Powell . . . to the black unemployed, homeless, and hungry of America's decaying urban ghettos—were philosophically, culturally, and racially the same. (p. 121)

Neomarxists raise important questions regarding the limits of Afrocentrism. Oyebade (1990) asserts that Marxist and Afrocentric theories can inform one another because they both are centered on the experiences of the oppressed. However, some Afrocentric scholarship rejects Marxist theoretical orientations outright. Asante (1987), for example, declares that "Marxism is not helpful in developing Afrocentric concepts and methods because it, too, is a product of a Eurocentric consciousness that excludes the historical and cultural perspectives of Africa" (p. 8). Neomarxist critiques, nevertheless, are useful given the bleak economic opportunities black people confront and they often provide an analysis of black life that highlight racial and economic justice issues (Marable, 1996). By refocusing on issues of social class, labor, and economic possibilities, Afrocentric reform can provide a powerful analysis of how both racial oppression and economic marginalization impact educational outcomes. Such analysis expands the current boundaries of Afrocentric reform and opens the possibilities for new questions about the capacity of Afrocentric theory and practice to improve the conditions of marginalized blacks.

Two

Hip-Hop Generation vs. Civil Rights Generation: The Challenge of Afrocentric Reform

RACE, CLASS, AND GENDER HAVE ALWAYS COMPLICATED ACCESS to public education in America. Questions regarding who should be educated and what type of education should be provided have presented serious challenges to public schools. For African Americans, the legacy of Jim Crow and decades of racial exclusion from quality education have undoubtedly created two educational realities. On one hand, education is a vehicle for social mobility and a higher quality of life. Yet on the other hand, education is a tool to reproduce social inequality. In the early 1970s, educators began to articulate the idea that access to quality education was necessary but insufficient. For these educators, education also meant new forms of representation in curricula that highlighted the importance of ethnic diversity (Sleeter, 1996).

Multicultural education promoted the need to include the cultural histories, experiences and learning styles of minority students. Since the early 1970s, there has been an effort on the part of textbook publishers, school districts, teachers, policy makers, and scholars to acknowledge and include an educational experience representative of all students and to promote the idea that Eurocentric biases in curricula put students of color at a learning disadvantage and damage their self- and cultural esteem (Hale-Benson, 1986; Kunjufu, 1985). Although there is substantial evidence that suggests this assumption is in part correct (Ladson-Billings, 1992), there is a tendency for scholars and practitioners to develop policies, strategies, and programs that simply celebrate students' cultures while failing to challenge or even acknowledge the oppressive conditions in which young people live. This approach also ignores the multiple and often complex identities of urban young people (McCarthy, 1995; McLaughlin, 1993) and undermines the profound influence that urban poverty has on

24

efforts to improve urban schools (Anyon, 1997; Connell, 1994; Noguera, 1996).

While multiculturalism strives to bring about racial equity in schools, its single-minded focus on ethnic and cultural identity fails to confront the complex economic challenges young people face. As a result, problems found in urban schools are often misdiagnosed (McCarthy, 1995). Although I agree that ethnic identity is an important feature in considering curricular reform, I argue that social class, economic conditions, and politics all work to shape efforts to improve urban schools.

AFROCENTRIC REFORM IN URBAN SCHOOLS

Afrocentric reform is an educational strategy designed to strengthen and improve the academic performance of students using principles based in ancient Egyptian culture. Afrocentric educators share four fundamental beliefs:

1. Unlike many other ethnic groups in the United States, the legacy of slavery disrupted the cultural continuity and disconnected enslaved Africans from an African identity and important cultural practices. As a result, African Americans in general and students in particular are disconnected from their African cultural roots that provide practices, beliefs, life lessons, and worldviews that are fundamental for cultural survival and success in school.
2. The persistent failure that black youth experience in schools is largely due to the cultural incongruence of the curricula they encounter. Afrocentric education is grounded on the "notion that culture influences all dimensions of human behavior, including teaching and learning" (Gay, 1994). Afrocentric reformers therefore believe that students who come from different ethnic, racial, and linguistic backgrounds than their teachers will experience cultural incongruence in the classroom, which in turn can lead to academic failure.
3. African culture (largely ancient Egyptian) provides a pathway to cultural practices that hold the promise for self-, social, and spiritual transformation. Many Afrocentric educators believe that through *Ma'at*—an ancient Egyptian worldview based on truth, justice, propriety, harmony, reciprocity, balance, and order—black students, in the process of reconnecting with African culture, can become more empowered.
4. Empowerment through African culture will translate to greater academic performance. This is accomplished by teaching students about African and African American contributions and culture, using teach-

ing techniques that are consistent with Ma'at, and creating curricula, across subjects, that are based on Afrocentric principles. Afrocentric education thus mitigates inconsistencies between the cultural backgrounds of teachers and black students. This belief has been summarized by Asa Hilliard as follows:

> Defamation of the name of a geocultural group creates psychological problems that can be addressed by rebuilding cultural identity (psychological health and mental liberation). Understanding and appreciation will occur if students learn the holistic and thematic history of geocultural groups. (quoted by Portland Public Schools, n.d.)

Afrocentric education has gained wide support as a promising strategy to remedy low academic performance in urban schools where black students continue to perform poorly. Educators have even pushed for the creation of entire Afrocentric schools rather then merely having Afrocentric curricula (Detroit Public Schools, 1992; Milwaukee Public Schools, 1990; Karp, 1991). This strategy was evident in the 1996 Ebonics debate over the Oakland Board of Education's approval of a plan to allocate funds to support "African Language Systems" designed to assist black students in mastering English language skills.

Proponents of Afrocentric education support the idea of replacing the universal Eurocentric approach to education primarily for African American students. While Afrocentric education is based on the worldviews and experiences of African and African American people, some Afrocentric educators highlight how Afrocentric strategies benefit both black and non-black students.

One of the first efforts to use Afrocentric strategies to seriously improve academic performance by bringing multicultural perspectives into classrooms was carried out in Portland, Oregon. In 1987, at the recommendation of Asa Hilliard, the Portland Public Schools commissioned the creation of the African American Baseline Essays, a series of texts that give information about the history, culture, and contributions of diasporic Africans in the areas of art, language arts, mathematics, science, social studies, and music (Klotz, 1993). The Afrocentric essays became required reading for all teachers in Portland's public school system.

The essays have become the centerpiece of other Afrocentric educational projects across the country. For example, in 1990, taking Afrocentrism in public schools one step farther, Detroit public school officials approved a plan to create three all-black, all-male schools as an effort to confront the lack of positive role models for black male students and improve the academic performance of African American students (Karp,

1991). Similarly, in 1992 school districts in Milwaukee and Baltimore began to investigate ways to implement African-centered curriculum into teacher training, curricula, and extracurricular activities.

Efforts such as these received wide support; and although they varied somewhat in their approach, they all shared three common characteristics. First, they all focused on African and African American contributions, history, and culture and were influenced by concepts outlined in Portland's Baseline Essays. Second, most of the Afrocentric reforms occurred in low-performing urban schools. Third, many of these schools were located in poor and working-class communities.

THE CHALLENGE OF AFROCENTRIC EDUCATION

Despite the fact that Afrocentric education is often used in poor and working-class communities, these strategies surprisingly have not adequately addressed the ways that poverty and class isolation impact young people's lives. Similar to other forms of multicultural education, Afrocentric reform views ethnic identity as the central mediator in the process of bringing equity into the classroom. As McCarthy (1988) notes, "The ideological and professional stance of multiculturalism therefore espouses an emancipatory program with respect to *racial* inequality in school [emphasis added]" (p. 268). Multicultural educational strategies such as Afrocentrism have almost exclusively focused on students' racial and cultural identities (Banks, 1993; Singer, 1994; Sleeter, 1996), while they have largely ignored the ways in which social class in general and poverty in particular have come to influence multicultural efforts in schools. The omission of such an analysis encourages simplistic models of black youth identity and avoids the complex intersection of class, gender, and sexuality and the rich variation within each group. McCarthy (1995) notes that educational theorists "treat racial groups as monolithic entities, disregarding both differences within groups and the interrelated dynamics of class and gender" (p. 272). In other words, most scholars tend to view racial groups, particularly urban youth, primarily by their racial composition, ignoring other potential elements of their identities. This type of analysis leads to an understanding of identity that is segmented, fragmented, and decontextualized.

One departure from racially informed scholarship is the work of Jean Anyon (1997). Anyon acknowledges the problems resulting from attempts to reform urban schools by considering the impact of both poverty and racial isolation. In her 4-year study of reforming eight public schools in Newark, New Jersey, she argues that urban school reform must be understood in the context of urban poverty. She reveals how the politics of race and class are embedded in the economic milieus of the communities where the schools are located. Unlike their suburban counterparts, urban schools are forced to grapple with the day-to-day reality of poverty, joblessness, and the consequent crime that has become common for poor communities. For many urban schools, the needs of their students far outweigh the meager resources available to them. The lack of basic school supplies and materials, deteriorating facilities, lack of parent involvement, and unprepared students all create greater challenges for schools in poor urban communities. She suggests that the difficulties that come with reforming urban schools often are a result of reformers not acknowledging the political, economic, and cultural realities within the communities where schools are located. Anyon forwards the idea that school reform must take into account these factors if we are to improve urban schools.

There are at least two implications for urban school reform from Anyon's analysis. The first implication is that schools are embedded within communities that have complex political and economic histories that shape and influence urban reform efforts. I call these *structural implications*. Structural implications involve understanding the ways in which economic factors, political decisions, and the public will come to play in changing urban schools and communities. This might involve understanding a long-term relationship between a grassroots organization and city officials. Similarly, it might involve understanding the economic history of a particular community in order to explain why and how a community changed from middle-class to poor and working-class. Structural implications are difficult to change but important to understand in urban school reform because they provide insight into how community histories and economic conditions shape reform efforts. For example, although it is highly unlikely that educational reformers alone could transform the economic conditions of a poor community, a clear understanding of structural implications could lead to a strategy that values working closely with stakeholders such as students, teachers, community residents, city officials, and private industry to transform both educational and economic conditions in a community.

The second implication of Anyon's analysis is that multicultural reform efforts often develop strategies with an incomplete picture of young people's identities (Anyon, 1995). I call these *sociocultural implications*. Sociocultural implications involve understanding the ways in which social class, race/ethnicity, and other components of identity influence reform efforts. For example, Anyon found sociocultural distances between reformers and students in an inner-city school. When she asked reformers and school officials if they had accounted for the fact that most of the children at the school were African American, they simply responded no.

Similarly, she inquired about the fact that most of the students at the school speak an urban "black dialect" of English. Again, the reformers had not considered how these factors might impact their efforts. Anyon suggests that reformers had little knowledge about the cultural and economic realities of the students who attended the school. She indicates that by not attending to youth identities, reform efforts "actually impede students' academic progress and thereby preclude reform success" (p. 77). Youth identities, however, are complex and are not simply defined by race or class alone. In fact, conceptualizing young people as having one dominant identity obscures the complex reality of their daily lives.

CONSIDERING BLACK YOUTH IDENTITY AND THE PROMISE OF HIP-HOP CULTURE

Reform efforts designed to strengthen academic performance through multicultural or Afrocentric strategies must be built on a more complete picture of black youth identities. Within the context of community, black youth identity can be thought of as a complex puzzle with many pieces— some large, others quite small, but all necessary to construct a complete picture. While social class and ethnic identity comprise a sizable part of this puzzle, other aspects of identity are also important. Sexuality, physical ability, and language all play a role in how urban youth construct their identities (McLaughlin, 1993). Identity, however, is also the product of resistance and struggle. Black youth in urban communities find themselves perpetually challenging racist stereotypes while at the same time struggling to find meaning and freedom in the context of racist public policies.

Haymes (1995a) illustrates that most whites believe that black youth and their schools are deeply racialized, disorderly, and dangerous. This notion of urban schools is promoted in popular culture by films like *Dangerous Minds* and *The Substitute* where urban schools are referred to as "battle grounds," "war zones," or even "the jungle." The image in these films of wild and untamed urban schools and communities justify having a white, civilized, ordered, disciplined, military-trained savior liberate racialized young people from their war-enthralled communities.

One of the most common ways that racist ideology is reified in urban schools is through public policy. For example, Davis (1996) exposed the ways in which public space in Los Angeles provided both protection from the urban poor and containment from perceived crime. In some urban schools, metal detectors and armed guards patrol the halls of these "violent" schools in order to maintain "safety" and "order," creating an almost prisonlike atmosphere.

Many black youth are pushed out of school and into prisons, resulting in significant social, political, and economic forces that shape the experiences and identity of all black youth. For example, in the wake of the crack epidemic during the 1990s, the term *black youth* became synonymous with *predator* (Males, 1996, 1999). Ideas such as the "war on drugs" and the "war on crime" ushered a public assault on black youth and their communities. Mike Males (1999) documented how xenophobic notions of youth as well as fear of crime helped shape public policy hostile to black youth during the 1990s. Despite the fact that youth crime had decreased since 1990, news stories continued to report "soaring youth crime" rates among black youth (We Interrupt This Message, 2001). Legislators responded by crafting public policy that underscored the idea that to be black, young, and poor was also to be criminal (Males & Macallair, 2000). These negative perceptions were reinforced through public policies that increased repression through institutions such as schools, law enforcement, and juvenile justice systems (Butts, 1999). From 1994 to 2000, for example, 43 states instituted legislation that facilitated the transfer of children to adult court. The result of these laws was the dismantling of a long-standing belief on the part of juvenile courts that special protections and rehabilitation were necessary to protect children and youth from the effects of the adult justice system. As a result, in 1996 African American youth were six times more likely to be incarcerated and received longer sentences than their white counterparts in Los Angeles County. When charged with the same violent crime, blacks were nine times more likely to be sentenced; for drug offenses they were sent to prison 48 times more often than whites charged with the same crimes (Poe-Yamagata & Jones, 2000).

Black youth in urban communities struggle to "not get caught up" in complex systems of control and containment, and their identities are often constructed in resistance to such racist stereotypes and unjust public policies. Their struggle for identity is played out through the expression of new and revived cultural forms such as hip-hop culture, rap music, and various forms of political or religious nationalism that redefine, reassert, and constantly reestablish what it means to be urban and black. These forms of identity are organic expressions of racial meaning that emerge out of a context of struggle within urban environments. For example, during the Black Power movement, the "Godfather of soul music," James Brown, captured the essence of the era for many urban blacks in the slogan "Say it loud, I'm black and I'm proud!" The term *Black Power* itself was coined by Willie Ricks and made popular by Stokely Carmichael, both leaders of the Student Nonviolent Coordinating Committee during the height of black frustration with the slow pace of the Civil Rights movement.

The common theme between all these expressions of black identity is that they all define blackness as a form of resistance. Black youth identity draws from the legacy of resisting white supremacist notions of blackness and reclaiming an identity that is rooted in everyday struggles. Omi and Winant (1995) remind us that construction of racial identity is a formative process and that social factors such as economic downturns, wars, and crime can alter racial meanings.

Today, urban reform efforts that focus entirely on ethnicity are insufficient. Reform efforts that attempt to improve the academic performance of black youth must consider economic, social, and political realities because they intimately shape the experiences of many poor and working-class black youth. For example, the Black Panther Party's popularity during the late 1960s and early 1970s was rooted not simply in cultural self-determination, but also on the capacity for thousands of black youth to identify with the party's struggle to improve their communities in the face of white-supremacist racial violence. For the Black Panther Party, reforming urban institutions such as the police department and schools was linked to larger economic and political issues of justice for the surrounding community (Hilliard & Weise, 2002; Newton, 1973). In a similar way, hip-hop culture provides today's black youth with an identity in opposition to racist public policy and oppressive urban conditions (Kelley, 1996; Kitwana, 2002).

Kitwana (2002) noted that the hip-hop generation (black youth who have grown up in the post– civil rights era) has witnessed corporate corruption, immoral religious leadership, and gross neglect of the plight of the poor on the part of politicians. Many youth of the hip-hop generation have lost faith in a system that seems to only protect the wealthy at the expense of their communities. This political perspective is key to black youth identity because it provides insight into the experiences, motivations, and aspirations of today's black youth, which are all necessary to connect with them in meaningful ways. Hip-hop culture provides not simply a voice for disenfranchised youth, but an identity that challenges racist practices, speaks to economic struggles, and sometimes provides a blueprint for the possibilities of social change (Kelley, 1996).

Hip-hop culture can be described as an emerging worldview among adults and youth born after 1965. This worldview is comprised of shared beliefs, practices, and language all tied together by a common appreciation for the urban aesthetic. Hip-hop culture shares at least two important characteristics. First is the urban youth aesthetic, which is perhaps the most easily recognizable aspect of hip-hop culture because it is expressed through music, clothing, language, and art. More than simply rap music and graffiti art, the urban youth aesthetic refers to visual and artistic expression of hip-hop culture. Rap music—expressive and innovative syncopated rhythms, laced with poetry, and story telling—was perhaps one of the first expressions of hip-hop culture during the early 1970s. The urban youth aesthetic is now a multibillion-dollar industry complete with clothing, art, language, and of course music.

Second is urban youth experience, which is often shaped by economic isolation, poverty, and a struggle to "make it out" of the trappings of urban ghettos. Hip-hop culture oftentimes validates, legitimizes, and celebrates experiences of violence, pain, fear, love, and hope that for urban youth are overlooked in mainstream America. To seriously discuss black youth identity, educators, policy makers, and researchers must consider the inseparable relationship between black youth identity and hip-hip culture. Failing to do so is a gross oversight.

BRIDGING THE GENERATION GAP: THE CHALLENGE OF THE NEW BLACK MIDDLE CLASS

Many black educators today, however, do not identify with or understand hip-hop culture. Kitwana (2002) notes that blacks from the civil rights generation cannot fully understand the complex modes of oppression confronting today's black youth. The removal of blue-collar work, the approval of legislation that has created an unprecedented number of incarcerated black males, and a burgeoning workforce that requires more specialized education have created a hostile environment that further marginalizes today's black youth. His observation points to how "the civil rights generation experienced segregation and second-class citizenship first-hand," and the antagonisms between black liberation and white supremacy offered an unambiguous analysis of oppression (p. 40). In contrast, oppression for the hip-hop generation is not "simply a line in the sand with white supremacist blocking access—us over here and them over there" (p. 4). Kitwana highlights the fact that the older generation's views of poverty, unemployment, and limited job options "exacerbate tensions between black youth and black adults because older black adults view poverty as simply something many of them overcame. Why can't your generation do the same? Or why does your generation use poverty as an excuse?" (p. 42). Because of these divergent views of oppression, many young black youth often see their own parents and other black adults as the enemy within the race.

This argument is also played out along class lines. Despite the fact that most middle-class blacks might have been poor once themselves, they now tend to view poverty as an inherent behavioral trait that is passed from one generation to the next (Hochschild, 1995). This phenomenon is attributed to the fact that middle-class blacks have deeply held beliefs about race and rarely call into question their own class privilege. Castells (1997) notes that "by and large, affluent African Americans do not feel welcome in mainstream society. Indeed, they are not. Not only racial hostility among whites continues to be pervasive, but gains by middle-class blacks still leave them way behind whites" (p. 56). Additionally, W. J. Wilson's (1996) research suggests that many middle-class blacks escape the inner city by moving to the suburbs and leaving behind masses of urban poor. As a result, many middle-class blacks are caught between being racially stigmatized by whites and viewed as removed and disconnected from their plight by poor blacks. Castells (1997) describes what motivates the actions of middle-class blacks:

> Most middle-class blacks strive to get ahead not only from the reality of the ghetto, but from the stigma that the echoes from the dying ghetto project on them through their skin. They do so, particularly, by insulating their children from the poor black communities (moving to suburbs, integrating them into white-dominated private schools), while at the same time, reinventing an African-American identity that revives the themes of the past, African or American, while keeping silent on the plight of the present. (p. 57)

Thus the black middle class experiences both racial exclusion from whites and class criticism from poor blacks. This in addition to the generation gap between their civil rights era and the hip-hop culture of the youth. As a result, black educators develop strategies that are out of sync with the most pressing issues confronting working-class black youth today.

PIECING THE PUZZLE TOGETHER

The challenge is to theorize about the ways in which multiple identities simultaneously inform one another. Perhaps the most significant contribution toward understanding the multidimensionality of identity is McCarthy's (1988, 1995) notion of parallelism. McCarthy argues against what he calls "new essentialisms" of race and proposes a framework that interrogates multiple forms of domination and attempts to explicate the ways in which race, class, and gender interact to reveal the complexity of identity formation. He maintains that "this framework . . . directs our attention to the interrelationships among a number of dynamics and that attempts to illuminate complexity, not wish it away" (1988, p. 272). He argues that identities are "products of human interests, needs and desires, strategies and capacities" and points to the contradictions and discontinuities that emerge from these multiple interests (1995, p. 250).

The point here is that identity, particularly as it relates to urban youth and working-class communities and schools, cannot be isolated from the struggles from which it emerges. Borrowing from Haymes (1995), McCarthy (1995), and Castells (1997), I argue that identity for poor black youth is largely tied to the everyday struggles found in their communities. It is the product of competing interests brought on by multiple forms of oppression; in the negotiation between these forms of oppression, black urban identity emerges. Hip-hip culture is central to conceptualizing black youth identity because it is an essential pathway to understanding their struggles, realities, and possibilities. While Afrocentric reform provides us with the necessary critique of race, it rarely confronts class, gender, age, sexual orientation, and so on. The multidimensional approach allows us to understand the ways in which black youth and their communities respond to oppression through the often unacknowledged strength, resilience, and resistance that emerges from alienation.

THREE

Black Life and the History of Oakland

THE BACKDROP FOR UNDERSTANDING THE AFROCENTRIC REFORM of McClymonds High School is Oakland, California. Oakland's history can be best understood in a context of economic ebb and flow, complicated by racial and class conflict. Since its early beginnings in 1850, Oakland has been a city of constant change and growth. Blacks first arrived in what is now known as Oakland as early as 1848 during the Gold Rush. One of the central issues facing blacks during this time was the issue of slavery prohibition. California, not yet an official state, debated over whether or not it would become a free or slave territory. Blacks taking great risks advocated not only for themselves but also for the abolition of slavery in the South as well (Crouchett, Bunch, & Winnacker, 1989). As a result, California did not allow slavery.

The culture of racial pride, social justice, and human equality indeed is rooted in the history of Oakland's black community. From the beginning, Oakland blacks struggled for American citizenship and exploited the few opportunities available to them. As early as 1857, Oakland boasted of its own private school for black children. By the end of 1860, blacks in Oakland had developed a small community with its own unique identity. Crouchett et al. (1989) note that by 1880 the black population in Oakland had grown to 593, which created a more complex social structure consisting of black churches, clubs, and fraternal organizations. These organizations provided the black community with both economic and social resources such as leadership from local churches and civic clubs. Crouchett et al. detail the political and educational struggle in Oakland that was evident as early as 1871 when the community of Brooklyn (now Oakland) restricted black children from attending its public schools. Being nearly a year without school, black parents in Oakland organized and sustained a campaign demanding that their children be admitted without restriction. The campaign was successful enough that in May 1872 the superintendent of schools for Oakland submitted this motion to the board of education: "At the opening of the school term in July, children of African descent may apply for admission to any of the public schools of the city of Oakland, and shall be received by the Principal of the school" (Crouchett et al., 1989, p. 5).

Black migration to Oakland prior to World War II occurred in four overlapping phases: demobilization following World War II (1945–1950); white flight and industrial relocation to the suburbs (1950–1975); deindustrialization (1975–1995); and most recently, demilitarization and base closures (1991–1995) (Lemke-Santagelo, 1997). Escaping the racist and oppressive conditions of the South, blacks began to arrive in Oakland in order to secure better work, improve their quality of life, and provide a better future for their children.

BLACK MIGRATION TO OAKLAND, 1869–1939

The first major wave of migration to Oakland began in 1869 when the Southern Pacific Transcontinental Railroad brought its West Coast terminus to Oakland. Soon after, the Pullman Company introduced sleeping cars for the long travel of its well-to-do customers. Each sleeping car required porters who provided a variety of personal services to passengers. Already serving and preparing meals and cleaning various facilities in and around the railroad, blacks (who usually served whites as maids or servants) seemed ideal for the job. Earnings of nearly $300 to $400 per month, the ability to travel, and the white-collar working conditions made being a Pullman porter a prestigious occupation among blacks. In fact, many Pullman porters were educated and well versed in European social etiquette. By company policy, a Pullman porter was a black man. Though this policy was restrictive and racist, it provided an opportunity for many black men to earn a handsome living and encouraged hundreds of black families to leave the South and relocate to West Oakland (Crouchett et al., 1989).

Later the Southern Pacific Company hired blacks to work as train yard laborers, baggage handlers, and waiters in dining cars, thus encouraging more blacks to migrate to Oakland for jobs and a better way of life. In 1870 there were 55 black residents in Oakland, but by 1880 that number had grown to 593. Crouchett et al. (1989) note that the railroad created a rapid expansion into the entire East Bay economy and generated a greater demand for new workers. Blacks were sought after to fill the gap that the Chinese and other local ethnic groups could not fill. Now a growing community, blacks in Oakland began to establish not only social clubs and churches, but even their own businesses:

> By 1870, blacks who had bought property in the preceding decades were able to realize great profits on their land, some of which they invested in

their own businesses. On the whole, these businesses were small, many offering services their owners had learned to perform as employees—barbershops, beauty salons, carpentry, painting establishments, dress shops, restaurants, retail shops, bars and clubs, and even small manufacturing. Between 1880 and 1890 the number of black men employed in Oakland more than doubled, and the variety of jobs in which they worked did likewise. (Crouchett et al., 1989, p. 13)

By the turn of the century, there were over a thousand black residents in Oakland. The San Francisco earthquake in 1906 contributed to the Oakland's expanding black population and to the growth of Oakland's black business. Largely due to racial discrimination in housing and in lending and employment practices, blacks created a strong cultural and economic community in Oakland. Concentrated primarily in West Oakland, a black business district began to take shape along Seventh Street. Barbershops, restaurants, cafes, billiards halls, and beauty salons lined the bustling black business district. Between 1900 and 1910 the number of blacks in Oakland nearly tripled, and by 1920 the number of blacks had exploded fourfold, becoming the city's largest ethnic group after whites (Bagwell, 1982; Crouchett et al., 1989).

The United States's entry into World War I in 1917 continued to provide Oakland blacks with jobs and financial stability for two reasons. First, the war provided more jobs through large industrial contracts for shipbuilding and heavy industry. The war also provided the canning industry with large contracts for food during the war. Second, the war drafted many factory workers—mostly white men—draining Oakland's industrial workforce. As a result of this labor shortage, companies were forced to hire black laborers to fill the void and keep up with the demanding production schedule created by the war (Bagwell, 1982; Crouchett et al., 1989; Davis, 1996). Crouchett (1989) notes that companies such as the Moore Shipbuilding Company along with "other industrial enterprises found themselves forced to hire black workers, who they had previously rejected on racial grounds" (p. 18).

The growing presence of blacks in Oakland spawned a backlash in the political and economic arena. Although there were few official sanctions on where blacks could live, de facto segregation restricted blacks primarily to West and later North Oakland. In 1930 the process for electing the city council from districts was replaced by at-large, citywide elections. This curtailed the potential power a black voting block could have on white elected officials. With less than 5 percent of the total population, black residents who had been able to trade votes for influence over council members from West and North Oakland for services and even administrative jobs were now without political representation (Crouchett et al., 1989).

Blacks in Oakland struggled, negotiated, and persevered through the depression until the early 1940s. Though many blacks were excluded from hiring during the massive federal relief programs that supported construction projects such as the San Francisco Bay Bridge, the Oakland Airport, and Treasure Island, blacks would not see another economic and population boom until World War II.

MIGRATION DURING AND AFTER WORLD WAR II

World War II had a profound effect on Oakland and its subsequent economic growth. Some have argued that World War II was the single most influential stimulus to the entire region since the Gold Rush (Bagwell, 1982). Shipbuilding and heavy industry again became the economic powerhouse of Oakland's wartime economy. Between 1940 and 1946, the federal government spent nearly $35 billion on wartime production in California alone. While Southern California's economy boomed with contracts from the aircraft industry, the Bay Area's swelled from shipbuilding contracts. Henry J. Kaiser, the engineer who constructed the Hoover Dam and the Bay Bridge, received numerous federal shipbuilding contracts and provided hundreds of jobs for East Bay residents. In addition to growth within the private industry, military installations in the Oakland area grew dramatically. The Oakland Naval Supply Center, the Oakland Army Base, and the Alameda Naval Air Station began to hire more civilians to cover additional workloads. By 1945, Oakland's population grew to over 400,000 with newly arrived families seeking employment in Oakland's wartime economy (Bagwell, 1982).

Among these new residents were once again blacks who were escaping the oppressive South for what seemed to be unlimited opportunity in California. Oakland's black population grew from 8,462 in 1940 to 37,327 in 1945 (Crouchett et al., 1989). Again, the growing presence of blacks in Oakland intensified racial hostilities. Union membership, closed shop practices, and outright overt racial discrimination became more commonplace for newly arrived blacks seeking employment. Whites in Oakland increasingly viewed the growing numbers of newly arrived blacks as a city problem, as described in *The Observer* of March 11, 1944:

> The riot on Twelfth Street the other day may be the forerunner of more and larger riots because we now have (a) a semi-mining camp civilization and (b) a new race problem, brought about by the influx of what might be called socially-liberated or uninhibited Negroes who are not bound by the old and peaceful understanding between Negro and the white in Oakland, which has

lasted for so many decades, but who insist upon barging into the white man and becoming a integral part of the white man's society. Thus we see, in Oakland, white women taxicab drivers serving Negro passengers, and white women waitresses serving Negroes in white men's restaurants. If that is not a source of trouble, we do not know what is. . . . the influx of the exuberant Negro has brought up the problem, and it is certain that the white man is not going to be pushed around in a civilization that is predominantly white. . . . It might be well for the more orderly and respectable Negroes to tell the newcomers about the facts of life. Otherwise we are going to have some more riots. (quoted by Bagwell, 1982, p. 240)

Despite the growing prosperity that many Oakland blacks experienced, they continued to bear the brunt of discriminatory practices in housing, employment, and education (Crouchett et al., 1989; Lemke-Santagelo, 1997). The NAACP documented discriminatory hiring and housing practices among some of Oakland's largest companies. Working with other local organizations, the NAACP charged companies like Chevron and Kaiser with discriminatory hiring practices. However, by 1944 the war boom had come to a halt, and blacks were left in an even more vulnerable position.

The economy shifted to accommodate peacetime efforts, leaving thousands of blacks unemployed. The common practice of the last hired being the first fired had taken its toll on thousands of black families in Oakland. By mid-1944, nearly one in every three black males in Oakland was unemployed (U.S. Bureau of Labor Statistics, 1950). To make matters worse, major employers such as Ford Motors, General Motors, and Borden Chemical, began to relocate from Oakland to surrounding areas such as San Leandro, Hayward, and Union City, seeking cheaper land, more space, and fewer union problems (Lemke-Santagelo, 1997). In 6 years—from 1958 to 1963—Oakland lost over 3,200 jobs, with other large employers set on leaving. With the exception of the Port of Oakland, nearly 30 percent of Oakland's manufacturing jobs had left by 1975 (Hayes, 1972; Lemke-Santagelo, 1997). The companies that did stay made the situation even more difficult for blacks by hiring whites from the suburbs for the higher paying jobs and excluding blacks from any work altogether. By 1985 Oakland had lost 24,000 jobs. As a result, mass unemployment for blacks was translated into a decrease in supporting black businesses that had been at the heart of Oakland's black community.

Despite the few job opportunities available to blacks in Oakland during the postwar period, blacks continued to migrate to Oakland. The black population in Oakland grew from 47,563 in 1950 to 83,600 in 1960. Though economically volatile, the black community in Oakland continued to grow until its political power could no longer be ignored. Various black organizations such as the NAACP fought against discrimination in employment, housing, and education. Refusing to return to the prewar days of white supremacy, blacks in Oakland retooled for a new era in politics and employment.

ECONOMIC DECLINE AND WHITE FLIGHT, 1945–1960

The impact of long-term unemployment was devastating to the black community. Unemployment among young black men rose from 28.6 percent in 1950 to 50 percent in 1970. What was once a bustling working-class community now faced massive unemployment and the beginning of systemic poverty (Crouchett et al., 1989; Lemke-Santagelo, 1997).

In addition to witnessing a mass relocation of major manufacturing jobs, Oakland also experienced what is now called *white flight*. Pushed from deteriorating facilities and expensive rents in Oakland and pulled by the attractive and inexpensive homes and plentiful job opportunities in the suburbs, whites began their exodus from Oakland as early as 1950. Rhomberg (1997) notes that in 1940 nearly 84 percent of the city's nonwhite population lived in 17 of the city's 72 census tracks. Most of these 17 census tracks were located in West Oakland. By 1950 the number of nonwhite residents in Oakland had more than tripled, but 90 percent of those residents occupied 16 census tracts. As indicated in Table 3.1, West Oakland was becoming rapidly an all-black community while whites were leaving. Between 1960 and 1970 Oakland's white population declined by 21 percent, while the city's black population increased by 41 percent. Within that decade, more than 42,000 whites fled Oakland for the surrounding suburbs (Lemke-Santagelo, 1997). The decline in white population continued until 1990 when whites made up only about 30 percent of the total population. See Table 3.1 for the ethnic makeup of Oakland's population from 1950 to 2000.

The shift in the racial composition of Oakland is complicated by the fact that discriminatory practices in housing eliminated the possibility for blacks in Oakland to relocate to the suburbs where many of the manufacturing jobs had gone. For example, in 1966 blacks made up less than 1 percent of the total population of Newark, San Leandro, San Lorenzo, and Union City combined (Hayes, 1972). Housing discrimination in the surrounding area became commonplace for both realtors and loan officers, making it nearly impossible for blacks to move out of Oakland. Lemke-Santagelo (1997) describes how the discrimination was carried out:

> Throughout the 1950s and 1960s the Southern Alameda County Real Estate Board steadfastly refused to share its property listings with Oakland's

Table 3.1. Oakland Population by Ethnicity, 1950–2000

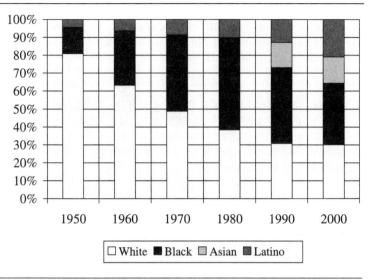

Sources: Association of Bay Area Governments, 1996; City of Oakland, 1994; U.S. Bureau of the Census, 2000.

integrated board of realtors, effectively denying information about available properties to prospective minority buyers. Agents and brokers, if approached by black clients, would steer them away from white neighborhoods, show property at inconvenient times or in less desirable locations, or simply fail to keep appointments. Lenders, too, discriminated against black buyers admitting that a "major factor" in loan eligibility is the location of the property. Banks frequently would refuse to make loans on some houses in certain areas, forcing applicants to go where lending rates are higher and more points are required. (p. 6)

Given the housing discrimination in the suburbs, the key to gaining access to employment was the availability of transportation to get back and forth to work. In 1966, however, public transportation to the surrounding suburbs was limited, and blacks were further alienated from the job market.

In all, there are three primary factors that contributed to the creation of Oakland's poverty during this period. First, there was a decline in manufacturing after World War II. Shipbuilding, steel manufacturing, and canning, which once comprised the mainstay of Oakland's economy, began to lay off workers as the demand for goods decreased. Being the last hired and first fired meant that blacks would be the first in the unemployment lines. Second, many of the manufacturing jobs were relocated from Oakland to the surrounding suburbs. Third, the discriminatory practices in housing made it increasingly difficult for blacks to move where the jobs were. As a result, thousands of blacks were left unemployed with little opportunity for meaningful work.

STRATIFYING THE BLACK COMMUNITY: THE CREATION OF OAKLAND'S BLACK MIDDLE CLASS

Despite the fact that Oakland's poor and unemployed continued to grow, some blacks were able to secure jobs that kept them from the unemployment lines. In fact, these blacks were able to enjoy limited financial mobility. Between 1960 and 1980, the black community in Oakland became more stratified along class lines. In the years prior to 1960, due to segregation and discrimination, most blacks in Oakland enjoyed a working-class lifestyle. After 1965, however, a substantial number of blacks experienced mobility into the middle class. After a decade of civil rights battles and antidiscrimination fights, some blacks were able to regain employment in manufacturing, metalworking, food packing, and equipment manufacturing. In fact, by 1960 the blue-collar sector—foremen, craftsmen, and laborers—employed proportionally more African Americans than any other group of workers (Lemke-Santagelo, 1997). Thus an interesting paradox emerged from this period.

In 1960 the median income for blacks in both San Francisco and Oakland was $2,712. By 1970, one out of every three black families in Oakland earned more than $10,000 a year. By 1970, the median income for black families in Oakland alone had more than doubled to $7,700. Similarly, the number of black families in Oakland earning between $15,000 and $25,000 more than tripled between 1970 and 1980. While Oakland blacks in 1970 held more than 56 percent of the jobs in the categories of professional, technical, managers and administrators, craftspersons, and service workers combined, they only made up 2.3 percent of the blue-collar workforce. Similarly, between 1970 and 1980, over 5,000 blacks entered white-collar professional occupations while during the same period nearly 3,000 black families fell below the poverty level (U.S. Bureau of the Census, 1973). In 1970 alone, 21.8 percent of all the black families in Oakland had incomes below the poverty level while at the same time 54 percent of all the black families had incomes at least twice that of the poverty level. Thus, while some blacks enjoyed the opportunity for social mobility, others remained unemployed and poor (U.S. Bureau of the Census, 1963; U.S. Bureau of the Census, 1973; L. J. Wilson, 1970).

What is evident here is the growing gap between Oakland's poor and working-class blacks and the new black middle class. This class schism occurred as Oakland retooled for a new global economy and shifted its major manufacturing jobs overseas, leaving thousands of blacks unemployed.

While private industry was primarily responsible for the creation of poverty among blacks in Oakland by the mass exodus of sustainable wage jobs, the federal government was primarily responsible for the creation of Oakland's black middle class. Between 1960 and 1975 the federal government expanded employment in Oakland by nearly 30 percent, employing nearly 30 percent of Oakland's black civilian workforce. The Alameda Naval Air Station, the Oakland Army Base, and Oak Knoll Naval Hospital, all of which employed blacks during the war years, continued to be an important source of jobs for blacks (Lemke-Santagelo, 1997).

By 1970, Oakland had two distinct black communities—one poor, the other middle-class—and each resided in different areas of the city (Brown, 1970). The poor primarily resided in what has become known as the "flatlands." Located between San Francisco Bay on the west and the Oakland hills on the east, the flatlands are comprised of low- to moderate-income residential housing. The black middle class, who had more flexibility due to income, either moved out of Oakland to the surrounding suburbs of Hayward, Union City, Vallejo, and Richmond, or moved into the Oakland hills area, which has moderate- to upper-income homes (Brown, 1970).

CLASS CONFLICT AND THE BATTLE OVER WEST OAKLAND COMMUNITY

West Oakland has always been a community under assault. Because of its unique location between downtown Oakland on the east and San Francisco Bay on the west, developers and community residents for years have battled over the future development of the community. For developers, the opportunity to redevelop ideally located property in an expansive economy has made West Oakland appealing to would-be investors. For residents of West Oakland, the community has been a place where powerful political and business leaders cut deals for economic gains while ignoring the needs of the community.

As early as 1949, West Oakland residents fought to stop the city from destroying the heart of the African American community located along Seventh Street. Seventh Street was home to numerous black-owned businesses, thriving shops and merchants who relied on the community for survival. However, by 1950 West Oakland lost over 25 percent of its homes and businesses to Urban Renewal through the construction of the Grove-Shafter and Cypress Freeways, displacing hundreds of families. The construction of the Cypress Freeway (Interstate 880) also split West Oakland into two separate communities and further isolated it from downtown. Thus the West Oakland economy was nearly destroyed.

By 1970, Oakland had forged a powerful black middle class comprised of lawyers, teachers, doctors, and numerous professionals which was large enough to wield considerable power over Oakland politics. Perhaps one of the most politically charged communities in Oakland has been West Oakland. In 1963, West Oakland was declared a depressed area under the federal Area Redevelopment Act. As a result, Oakland qualified for federal assistance through the federal government's poverty programs directed at reducing poverty in designated neighborhoods in Oakland. The target areas in Oakland were North Oakland, West Oakland, Fruitvale, and East Oakland (Rhomberg, 1997). Additionally, substantial federal dollars were tied to urban redevelopment that added to the ensuing conflicts that often split along race and class lines. It is within the context of urban renewal and Oakland's poverty programs that we begin to see conflict along class lines within the city's black community.

A series of major conflicts emerged beginning in 1964 when Mayor Houlinhan began to appoint members to the newly formed Oakland Economic Development Council (OEDC) which would be responsible for overseeing how the new federal dollars would be spent. Nine of the 25 appointees were black and represented the interests of business and private industry. There was a stipulation in the federal grant, however, that required the overseeing agency (OEDC) to be comprised of residents of the target areas of Oakland. Because none of the black appointed members resided within any of the target areas, OEDC was forced to recruit residents within the target areas. In 1965, they formed the Target Area Advisory Committees (TAACs) who would carry out the plans of OEDC and would have a representative from each target area serve on the OEDC. The membership of target area committees varied, but they were largely black, Latino, and low-income (May, 1973). Rhomberg (1997) notes characteristics of the TAACs:

As TAACs became more active, differences began to emerge. . . . For their part, working class members of the TAACs held a different view of their role and of the best strategy for the fighting of poverty. They had much less faith in established institutions and in any new services that these might provide. They believed that what the poor needed most were immediate direct benefits, like jobs, legal aid, and child care, not technical assistance and referral services, or education programs (like Head Start) aimed exclusively at future generations. They were less interested in coalescing with other sectors, and preferred self-help programs that they could run themselves. Frustrated by their inability to hold the more educated and professional at-large members accountable, they believed that for their own protection, they should properly control the OEDC. (p. 221)

The target area members articulated the problems people in their communities confronted very differently than the black middle-class OEDC members. TAAC members saw poverty needing to be addressed by direct, immediate, and concrete solutions such as employment and child care. They articulated the problems from the stance of knowing what people in their communities wanted and needed most. The black professional members of OEDC, however, sought to strengthen the existing institutions within these communities such as the school district and various municipal employment agencies. OEDC accommodated TAAC concerns when the Ford Foundation announced that it would distribute $600,000 to indigenous groups through OEDC (May, 1973; Rhomberg, 1997). As the TAACs began to jockey for more power within OEDC, more conflict emerged.

In September 1965, OEDC voted to expand its membership, prompting members of the TAACs to propose that at least 50 percent of the membership of OEDC be comprised of low-income residents of the target areas. Taking the matter even further, the TAAC from the Fruitvale area included a list of demands, which required, "51 percent low-income membership, the right to review proposals, and that requirements for staff jobs not be limited as to exclude residents without formal education or professional training" (May, 1973; Rhomberg, 1997, p. 226).

Although the middle-class blacks in OEDC "defended their leadership over the poverty programs, despite their high incomes and residence outside the target areas, by referring to their own personal origins and memories of growing up in the ghetto" (Rhomberg, 1997, p. 226), TAAC members clearly understood the class differences between OEDC leaders and themselves. The low-income residents were critical of programs that allocated large amounts of money to established institutions and professional staff salaries when residents needed jobs and income. "They based their own authenticity on the fact of their ongoing everyday experience and knowledge of the neighborhood" (p. 227).

The most poignant difference in this conflict is how each constituency articulated the "poverty problem." For OEDC's black middle-class, poverty was seen as a consequence of both personal pathology and economic decline. The solution for OEDC lay in motivating the poor to work, providing job training, and strengthening existing institutions. The assumption among OEDC members was that existing institutions had both the capacity and the will to provide the necessary resources for poor and working-class blacks. For poor and working-class members of TAACs, the problem was clear: Provide jobs, day care, and other immediate solutions and allow the people who live in and best understand the community to manage the process. By 1966 the TAACs had won majority control over OEDC and residents of poor neighborhoods had taken control of Oakland's poverty programs.

The class conflict here represents the ways in which national movements and initiatives articulate themselves at the local level. In Oakland the federal government's War on Poverty programs made explicit the class differences within the city's black community. Accompanying the differences between the classes are ideologies that emerge from one's class experience. For Oakland's black middle class, this meant an understanding of poverty that both supported their class position and attempted to gain legitimacy from the poor by reaching back to the days of "growing up in the hood." For the poor and working class, their understanding of poverty was based on everyday lived experiences. What is key for this conflict is the way in which power over the distribution of federal dollars transitions from OEDC's middle class to TAACs' poor and working-class constituents.

WEST OAKLAND TODAY

From 1960 to 1966, approximately 18 percent of the housing stock in West Oakland was lost in the course of a series of redevelopment measures. The closure of the Naval Base, along with several large manufacturing plants, has prompted the departure of many working-class residents (Gushiken, Hillmer, & Noguera, 1988; Noguera, 1996; Coalition for West Oakland Revitalization, 1994). Additionally, the mass removal of federally subsidized housing known as ACORN has further displaced and dispersed hundreds of West Oakland families throughout the East Bay.

In West Oakland today there is an obvious absence of essential retail services such as banks, grocery stores, and drug stores. The last grocery store in West Oakland, Acorn Supermarket, charged 36 percent more for lesser quality produce than other grocery stores in Oakland. The majority of building and office space along West Oakland's major streets are vacant and in poor physical condition. West Oakland has some of the city's oldest homes in the city; 63 percent of the homes were built before 1959. The community contains 1,359 vacant and boarded structures, which comprise nearly 7.5 percent of the entire city's vacant lots.

While the community remains a poor, working-class community, West Oakland continues to recover from its history of redevelopment and economic displacement. The 1989 Loma Prieta earthquake destroyed the Cypress freeway as well as homes and commercial buildings in the area. Considerable community pressure has prompted the city to rebuild the Cypress freeway so that it would not split West Oakland. In June 1998, nearly 10 years later, the freeway was reopened and now channels traffic around West Oakland with key street exits that make it easier to travel in and out of the community.

Current redevelopment efforts call for more neighborhood stability, community activity, employment, and economic revitalization of the Seventh Street corridor, which was once the economic heart of Oakland's black community. All these efforts will benefit from the construction of the new freeway.

On November 14, 1998, the "kick off" of the Seventh Street McClymonds Corridor Improvement Initiative drew nearly 300 West Oakland community residents, politicians, and community organizers. The initiative is a 7-year project aimed at improving the physical, economic, and human conditions in West Oakland. By using leaders within the existing community (pastors, educators, parents, and other residents), the project seeks to develop and implement strategies that strengthen the capacity for West Oakland revitalization. Funded by the William and Flora Hewlett Foundation and managed by the San Francisco Foundation, the project also increased and improved coordination of existing services and programs available to West Oakland residents. Since 1998, the Seventh Street McClymonds Corridor Improvement Initiative has distributed over one million dollars in funds to local nonprofits to provide comprehensive and coordinated services to the West Oakland community. Some of the project accomplishments include a shuttle service for seniors to social service and commercial destinations, a credit union with over 500 members and more than $2.5 million in economic resources, and support for 12 different youth development programs that provide hundreds of West Oakland youth with after-school activities, including multimedia training, leadership, development, and arts education.

Four

Oakland Schools in Crisis

IN 1985 JAMES GUTHRIE FROM THE UNIVERSITY OF CALIFORNIA completed a comprehensive study of Oakland Unified School District (OUSD). Hired by the school board as a consultant to identify major problems within the district, the report highlighted what many residents of Oakland had already known—OUSD was in trouble and needed an overhaul. According to the report, Oakland schools were among the worst in the country and the students performed well below national averages (Guthrie, 1985). The comprehensive study examined aspects of management, teaching, curriculum, and finances and found 18 major areas where the district had failed both students and the community:

1. Unacceptably low levels of student achievement
2. High dropout rates
3. Too few secondary academic course enrollments
4. Students' delusions regarding quality of their schooling
5. Eroded public confidence
6. Increasing enrollments
7. Growing numbers of limited-English-speaking students
8. Professional vs. parent "fight"
9. Absence of an effective personnel evaluation system
10. Large classes
11. Low teacher morale
12. Shrinking dollar resources
13. Inadequate pupil performance measures
14. Ineffective management systems
15. Poor policy-setting procedures
16. School board–administration conflict
17. Misallocated fiscal resources
18. Inadequate systems for monitoring district performance

For years the district had struggled with the dilemma of how to improve the educational experience for its majority ethnic student population. A common perception among some residents of Oakland was that the schools did not serve the needs of their children and that they needed much improvement. Many of the district's schools performed well below national averages on several standardized tests. Additionally, a report subtitled *Sounding the Alarm on Suspensions,* produced by the Urban Strategies Council in Oakland (Commission for Positive Change, 1992), exposed the district's disciplinary policy and revealed that it had disproportionately discriminated against black and Latino males. Taken together, these helped fuel growing community discontent with the district. Some principals and administrators within the district, however, resisted community pressures to change, charging that the community folks weren't the experts. An administrator for the school district related an incident in which parents were at odds with administrators:

> I think the perception is that we are in the process of change. And that positive changes are not happening rapidly enough for the betterment of our students. We're not doing well to improve student achievement for all of our students. I also think the perception is, that we can't improve because of the political climate. . . . We had a principals' meeting yesterday, and this task force [consisting of parents and teachers] made the presentation to the principals yesterday, and they said it was going to be in the media today, the article. And principals were most upset, and I agree with them. How can you call a press conference, call the media in, when you have not discussed the task force recommendations with us? The principals are the people who are going to implement these recommendations. The principals also felt that the people who made the presentation to the group should not have been a parent and a teacher. You mean to tell me that we have to get this from a parent? We have to get this from a teacher, when we're supposedly the leaders and the educators. Now I think that's the political climate. I think administrators have not taken a strong stand by saying that "I'm the educator, and I'm the professional person, and I know what I'm doing." Somehow we have given that over to others, for whatever the reason might be.

Ongoing tension between community residents, school administration, and teachers has contributed to the lack of faith in Oakland Public Schools. Over the past 2 decades, the district has had four major teacher strikes causing the schools to close early or delay the start of the academic school year (Cunningham, 1996). For the third time in 4 years, teachers went on strike in 1995 to increase salaries and renegotiate the teacher's union contract (Bazeley, 1995; Li, 1992; Olszewski, 1996; Wagner, 1996).

Though unacknowledged, another perception about the district is that its diverse racial makeup contributes to the ongoing low academic performance. Since 1984, African American students have held the majority in Oakland Public Schools with 54 percent of the student body; the rest of the students are Hispanic, 17 percent; Asian, Filipino, and Pacific Islander, 18 percent; and white, 8.3 percent (OUSD Department of Research and Evaluation, 1992). For many community residents, Oakland Public Schools is considered to be a predominately black school district. This perception comes from a majority black student population, a majority black school administration and support staff, and a majority black school board. While racial inequities clearly exist in the school district, the perception of a predominately black school district makes it more difficult to attribute the schools' problems to racial discrimination and exclusion. Adding to community frustration, then, was the fact that even in a predominately all-black district student performance continued to suffer.

In fact, the Guthrie report surveyed perceptions of the school district and found that nearly 25 percent of all the parents surveyed gave their students' high schools a D or F grade. The teachers who worked for the district were even more critical of Oakland's high schools. Over 35 percent of the teachers survey gave Oakland high schools a D or F grade (Guthrie, 1985). The Guthrie report confirmed these perceptions among parents, community, and educators. By comparing OUSD with similar districts, the report revealed that other similar large districts in California outperformed Oakland on standardized achievement tests. Table 4.1 compares Oakland with four urban California school districts based on an index of scores from students with similar socioeconomic backgrounds. Students in districts above the "0" line scored higher than expected of them based on students' socioeconomic background, but Oakland students consistently scored below expectations (Hytha, 1985).

Hytha (1985) noted that "Oakland students also lacked less tangible but crucial language skills not measured by standardized achievement tests. Employers commented that many Oakland students do not even know how to fill out the most basic job application" (p. 5). The state of OUSD was complicated by the fact that 83 percent of the seniors believed they were "being well trained for jobs or further education" (p. 5). To make matters worse, the report revealed an ineffective "bloated" administration with numerous staff positions.

While many school administrators approached the report as a challenge to improve the failing district, it was still damaging to the district's national and statewide image. Additionally, even though the commu-

Table 4.1. Student Achievement Among Similar California School Districts, 1998

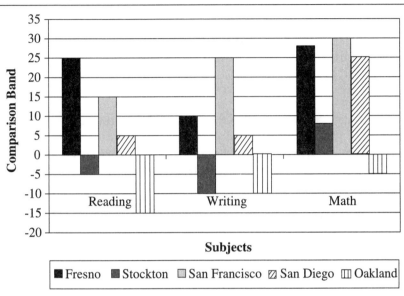

Adapted from M. Hytha, 1985.

nity had already lost faith in the district, the report opened a "Pandora's box" for community complaints and criticisms. One community resident recalled:

> We found that the school district was tracking black kids off into the, what we call the "skill courses," . . . [but] all of those tests come . . . [from] the content of the curriculum of the university track. And you track a kid over here in what you call the below average track or the skills track there, and you don't expose him to the proper curriculum that prepares him to be able to compete . . . naturally he's going to fail. And in the process once he fails, then he ends up becoming not qualified to go into the college, he's not qualified to go into the job market, he's not qualified to go into the zoo. And naturally . . . he can't go into business for himself, because he hasn't been exposed to the quality of content of the curriculum that would prepare him to do these things.

Community residents of Oakland were acutely aware of the consequences of poor education for their children. They knew that poor education would lead to a continued cycle of poverty and few opportunities for financial mobility. Ultimately, the report added fuel to the community pressure to improve the ailing school district. Growing community concern about the operation of Oakland's schools was buttressed by constant scandal within the district.

DISTRICT CORRUPTION AND STATEWIDE FISCAL TURMOIL

To make matters worse, from 1985 to 1989 OUSD had been involved in numerous lawsuits ranging from embezzlement and sexual harassment to outright theft. Nearly everyday the newspaper reported on a new scandal within the district (Grabowicz, 1989; Grabowicz & Frost, 1989a, 1989b, 1989c; Harris, Grabowicz, & Frost, 1989). A district administrator and former principal recalled the turmoil the district was involved in:

A lot of scandal was reported in the newspaper about the district. Mismanagement, fiscal mismanagement. People were stealing from the district. People were filling out false time sheets, all kinds of stuff went on.

In December 1988 Joe Coto, the district's superintendent, resigned his post, leaving the district without a superintendent for almost a year. By 1989 the troubled district was fraught with problems such as low student achievement, fiscal problems, and widespread theft and corruption. As a result, the district was placed under state control in September 1989 by the state Superintendent of Public Instruction, Bill Honig. It wasn't until November 1989 that the board of education hired Richard "Pete" Mesa to fill the vacancy (Frost, 1989a, 1989b).

Mesa accepted the position fully aware of the problems he would confront. OUSD faced severe budget problems. Nearly $8.2 million short, Mesa was faced with the task of orchestrating major budget cuts (Cutler, 1993). The OUSD budget shortage was amid a decline in state revenues and a major recession in California. By June 1989, California had cut major dollars from state spending creating drastic shortages in local schools and municipalities. The state cuts meant a 34-million-dollar deficit for Oakland, and as a result, the city manager along with mayor Elihu Harris called for a salary freeze for all city employees, most of whom had not had a cost of living increase for 2 consecutive years. Of all the public institutions in the city, Oakland Public Schools was hardest hit by California's economic crisis. Mesa indicated during a meeting of educators in June 1992 that the 3.8-billion-dollar decline in state revenues combined with the decrease in lottery funds and possible reductions of categorical programs would have a devastating impact on the district. In fact, state funding provided 95 percent of the revenues for general purpose funds in Oakland Public Schools. The other 5 percent was made up of lottery and federal dollars. Furthermore, Mesa explained that 2 years before, the lottery had provided $173 per student, but during the 1992–93 academic year, the lottery only provided $83 per student.

Mesa tried to assure parents and other community residents that the cuts would be kept as far away from the classroom as possible. He proposed cutting nearly $2.3 million from the office administration and another $225,000 from annuities. He argued that these cuts would have minimal impact on classroom instruction and important programs for students. Mesa stated, "This budget incorporates the most recent information of the District's financial status, with the possibility that additional adjustments may be required as a result of the governor's budget" (Atkins, 1992a, p. 1). To no avail, community residents and parents responded to Mesa and the school board's proposed budget with reservation. The president of the Oakland Education Association, Ward Roundtree, began by accusing Mesa of not being open and honest about Oakland schools' financial situation, indicating that it only contributed to the school board credibility problem in the community. He stated, "Do what it takes to provide a quality education, and put out information in a way that people will have faith in the district" (Atkins, 1992b, p. 1). A history of low academic performance, recent stories of financial mismanagement, and now financial crisis contributed to the community's distrust of the school board. Roundtree's comments were followed by applause from the audience and opened the meeting to other comments from concerned community residents. One resident told the board members "they had gotten too far removed from the community into the hills to be understood by the community." He asked them "to take off the ties and sophisticated attitudes and organize marches that should go to Sacramento" (Atkins, 1992a, p. 1).

These community responses represented a common sentiment among some community residents that the board had forgotten the "flatlands" and had become disconnected from the actual struggles of the working-class community. This comment also pointed to the fact that even though the board racially represented the community (5 black, 1 Latino, 2 Asian), they did not properly represent the working-class community. Though some members of the school board were known for their commitment to working-class concerns, the perception among some residents was that the board as a whole had forgotten the struggles of working-class people.

More important, the district had become vulnerable to state and local community pressure. The state budget crisis along with drastic cuts in educational spending in the school district created an environment of distrust in the community who wanted to see more being done to improve the educational opportunities for their children. The community's distrust was supported by allegations of ongoing scandal and mismanagement within the district. Lawsuits and the outright removal of high-level officials contributed to a strong sense that the board and the district could care less about the schools and the children who attended them.

COMMUNITY PERCEPTIONS OF MCCLYMONDS HIGH SCHOOL

The 1993–94 school year represented the fourth consecutive year the district was forced to make substantial budget cuts. In the previous 3 years alone, the district had cut nearly $50 million from various programs and administrative services. This year Mesa could not commit to leaving the schools out of the budget cuts; he stated, "It is harder every year to find any fat to trim from the budget. . . . this is the first year since I am here that we have had to cut programs close to students" (Cutler, 1993). After reviewing which vital programs and services were needed for the district, Mesa recommended to the board of education giving school district staff 2-day furloughs, the removal of several administrative posts, closing three area administrative offices, and closing two schools.

Once again Roundtree, the teachers union representative, criticized Mesa's proposal for not putting students first. He presented a proposal that prioritized students and their most basic educational needs (teachers, materials, facilities, and so on). With more complaints from parents, the board indicated that the decision to shut a school down would be based on the capacity to hold the children, the condition of the school, the condition of the facilities to provide the best programs, and the distance children would travel.

These criteria made McClymonds High School an ideal candidate for closure. Since the late 1980s in fact, there had been discussion by the district to close McClymonds due to continued decline in enrollment, high dropout rates, high rates of suspension, and the lowest academic performance in the district. The problems at McClymonds or "Mac" had earned it the title among many educators as the "worst school in Oakland." A former principal of McClymonds commented:

> I've been associated with McClymonds for a long time, in fact since 1969, when I went to McClymonds as head counselor. At

that time, the enrollment was between 950 and 980, and the population was mostly all black, with a staff that had been somewhat stable throughout the years, as I understood it. Quite a young staff at the time, when I went there, including myself. So we had a lot of energy, and put forth a lot of effort to make things better for the kids. In 1973, there was some dissatisfaction with McClymonds, in that we—the staff, the community—were not moving forward as we should, as far as student achievement and as far as preventing the dropout rate. I returned to McClymonds in 1983, and at that time the enrollment was approximately 850. Many of the staff members were still there. They were sort of disenchanted, because of a number of things. The dropout rate was beginning to rise again and the student enrollment had dropped. The staff felt that they were not supported by the district and [were not] getting some of the things that they wanted, including materials, including support personnel. . . . McClymonds unfortunately has had a reputation for many, many years, even before I became connected to the school in 1969, in that people perceived McClymonds as the worse school in Oakland. The perception was very strong, and it certainly filtered over to the school community.

In fact, from 1989 to 1993 McClymonds's annual enrollment had dropped by 15 percent. By 1995 enrollment was down to 632 and the dropout rate had risen from 11 percent in 1992 to 24 percent in 1994 (see Table 4.2). Making matters worse, McClymonds had the highest suspension rate in the district at 28 percent in 1992–93 (see Table 4.3).

While "Mac" had once been known for its academic and athletic excellence, it had become a school plagued with problems. By 1990 the school was nearly out of control. Teachers and counselors recalled that students and nonstudents would come and go as they pleased, hang out and smoke in the hallways, and cause major disruptions. Nearly everyday someone would set off the fire alarm. One teacher recalled several incidents where students would set garbage cans on fire inside the school corridors. One community resident commented about some of the problems the school had experienced.

McClymonds had gone down. Students were not coming to school, and when they did come to school they just hung out in the halls and openly used drugs, there was no accountability. Everyday there were fights and lots of young girls were getting pregnant, it was in bad shape.

Table 4.2. Dropout Rates in Oakland High Schools, 1992–1994

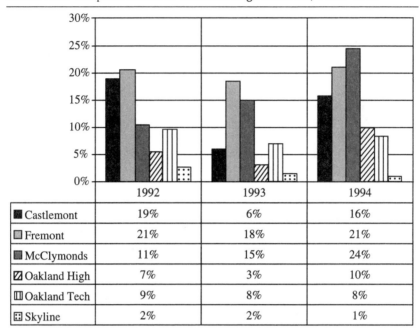

	1992	1993	1994
■ Castlemont	19%	6%	16%
▢ Fremont	21%	18%	21%
▨ McClymonds	11%	15%	24%
▨ Oakland High	7%	3%	10%
▥ Oakland Tech	9%	8%	8%
⊞ Skyline	2%	2%	1%

Note: Students are reported as dropouts if they are absent 45 consecutive days and no transfer of records has been requested for them.

Source: Oakland Unified School District, Department of Research and Evaluation, 1996a.

A former student from McClymonds recalled that the school was "off the hook" meaning that students enjoyed the freedom to do what ever they wanted, including hanging out in the halls, and smoking marijuana:

> The students who were there [at McClymonds], I don't think they really took it seriously. Like what I heard from the students before I was there was, you know, "Mac was off the hook," you know, they had another principal. . . . There was a lot of nonsense going on. . . . smoking in the hallways. People just really cutting class. People would just be cutting out, you know, not taking care of business up there. And they, you know, the principal, he wasn't as strong as the principal we have now, so I guess he let a lot of it go on. But it was just wild, basically.

Table 4.3. Suspension Rates in Oakland High Schools, 1990–1993

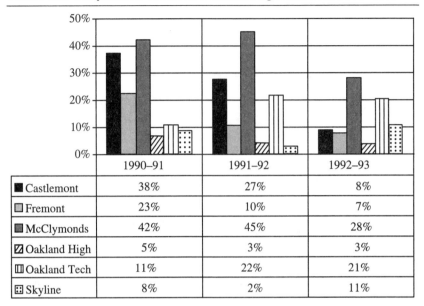

	1990–91	1991–92	1992–93
■ Castlemont	38%	27%	8%
▢ Fremont	23%	10%	7%
■ McClymonds	42%	45%	28%
▨ Oakland High	5%	3%	3%
▥ Oakland Tech	11%	22%	21%
▦ Skyline	8%	2%	11%

Source: Oakland Unified School District, Department of Research and Evaluation, 1996a.

Another student commented that in comparison to her previous school, McClymonds students did not seem to care about their education. In fact, it appeared that for some students the school was primarily a place to go hang out during the day when they had nothing else to do.

> I come from a school, a predominantly white school, where everyone was about taking care of business, and you could, you were more into taking care of business and doing what you had to do, you know, because you were around a positive crowd. . . . When I came to McClymonds, if you tried to take care of business and do what you had to do, and be positive, you, I mean, you were one out of the few. . . . They came to school just to, you know, hang around, or just to smoke. . . . They didn't look at McClymonds like the educational institute like it should've been looked at. And I just, I thought it was very negative.

While the school grappled with its academic problems, it also suffered from deviant student behavior, rampant drug use during school hours, and lack of parental involvement. Some parents were so disconnected from both their children and the school that there was little recourse the school could take. As a consequence, many of these students were expelled or suspended.

PARENTAL INVOLVEMENT

Lack of parental involvement was the result of a complex relationship between economic variables like unemployment and social conditions like drug use. In order to best understand the lack of parental involvement, one must also examine the context in which it emerged. For some families, the day-to-day struggles to "make ends meet" with limited work often overshadowed requests to get more involved at McClymonds. For other families, the devastating impact of the drug trade had a profound impact within schools (Payton, 1989). For example, among children seen in the Alameda County juvenile court system, 85–95 percent had parents who used drugs. As a result of either court mandate or county child protective services, nearly one out of every ten students (ages 10 to 17) in Oakland did not live with either parent (Urban Strategies Council, 1996). An estimated 3,200 youth took up residence with relatives: grandparents (1,100), brothers or sisters (1,000), or aunts and uncles (1,100). Most common, however, was foster care and residential placement which often filled the void of parents who had become victims of drug use (see Figure 4.1). Not able to care for their children, these parents rarely were able to be involved with their child's

Figure 4.1. Oakland Youth in Foster Care by Race, 2000

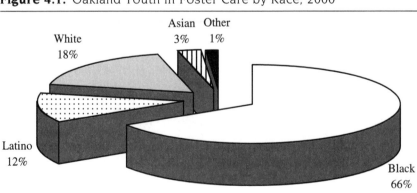

Source: Alameda County Social Services, 2000.

schooling. A school counselor who worked at McClymonds for four years commented on parents and the lack of parental involvement:

> If I see a parent I'll talk to them, if they need some help, but usually you don't really see them. It's not like we have like a strong PTA or anything here at McClymonds. But I think that is because of the ages of some of the parents. Most of them were teen parents and stuff like that, so they're kind of now getting into their own life, becoming adults and doing their own thing. You know, "My kid's a little older, I can go kick it," you know, type thing. Or they are working so hard that they don't have time to, you know, come to the school to do things. . . . Or they're not even present, because a lot of teens, too, live with grandparents or aunties or uncles and stuff like that. . . . They might have gotten taken away from their parents because of [their parents'] substance abuse and neglect. [Or] they didn't, don't get along with their parents so then they end up going to stay with another relative. Or, you know, that kind of stuff.

Thus while some parents attempted to get involved with the school, the majority remained on the periphery. A recent graduate of McClymonds commented on her experience in West Oakland and the parental involvement of her peers' parents:

> Poverty is a big part, you know—drugs, and parents on drugs. That is such a big problem. A lot of my peers, you know, that I've known, you know, have parents who are on drugs, are being raised by their grandparents, or by somebody, you know, a family member or a family friend. A lot of kids, you know, a lot of parents are just lost. That whole drug epidemic, you know, just really, really destroyed a lot in our community that we're still suffering from it. And so, you know, in response to that, you have kids with not much parental guidance, and [not] much, you know, influence, inspiration, role models, and so they fall off track. Some of them have even been exposed to drugs, and that's why they find themselves not being able to concentrate or learn very quickly.

LIVING IN WEST OAKLAND

Poverty in West Oakland even further impacted the school. During the 1990–91 school year, the number of students whose families qualified for

AFDC (Aid to Families with Dependent Children) was the highest in the district at 135 percent. The number of school-aged AFDC children living in the census tract served by these schools exceeds the enrollment of the school. The unemployment rate in West Oakland in 1990 was 9 percent while 53 percent were not included in the labor force at all (OCCUR, 1990; Urban Strategies Council, 1995, 1996). A student at McClymonds reflected on the poverty of her community:

> A lot of kids are coming from homes where they don't have that much food. You know, they're—a lot of these kids even have to go work to support their families, sometimes. I mean that's not new to us, you know. That's been going on all through our history. But West Oakland is a low-income area, basically. I'm not sure of the exact statistics, but there's a good number who, of children who are being raised on welfare, a good number of parents who are unemployed, and that, you know, that creates a lot of problems.

Virtually no retail stores exist in West Oakland and many of the residents are forced to travel long distances for basic grocery items because West Oakland's only grocery store has been closed since 1996. A teacher at McClymonds and a West Oakland resident described how the community has changed since the 1970s:

> We used to have a lot of doctors and lawyers that lived in our community. They all moved out. They rent out their places now. ... When I show them the history of West Oakland, and I show them where the BART station is, how that used to be shops and parlors, you know, shoeshine parlors and grocery stores and butcher shops and a pharmacy, and they say, "Oh, man, that's all there." They see that, and I say, "And it was all black-owned." And the kids look at that, and I say, "Now, you see what's happening to your community? Everything has been taken out." You go down there now, you look at, Acorn's half torn down now, and all that kind of stuff. Acorn Supermarket hasn't been open [since 1996]. ... They say, "Your people don't spend big money, they don't come in and spend $200, $300. They spend $10 and come back the next day." ... They want their big supermarkets, you know. That's corporate America. You know, I understand that. But how come the closest supermarket we have, you have to go way to Emeryville, to

Pack'n'Save? And now a lot of them go there. No ATMs and
no pharmacy.

At McClymonds High School, as at other schools throughout the city,
the poverty and the influx of drugs was complemented with increased
violence and homicide among poor youth. In 1990 homicide was the leading cause of death among Oakland youth aged 10–24. Between 1989 and
1994 nearly 410 African American youth lost their lives to gun violence
(Urban Strategies Council, 1996). Fights and even gun violence became
almost commonplace to McClymonds students. When the new principal,
Mr. Hamilton, came to the school, the behavior of the students was so trou-
bling that it prompted him to carry a video camera with him wherever he
went so that he could videotape and document nearly every occurrence
of misbehavior. He said that the reason behind recording these students
was that he could use it as evidence in case he needed to have them leave
the school. According to Hamilton, students know that when they are on
film it becomes official, so they either stop misbehaving or leave.

Mrs. S., a caseworker from an outside agency who had been assigned
to work with pregnant and parenting students at McClymonds, commented
on a conversation she had with a student.

> The other day the principal brought a student into my office. She
> wanted to transfer because she was saying that she was getting into
> too many fights, and she didn't want to be here. . . . She talked
> about how her stepfather had been beating her mom, and how
> she'd missed a lot of school because she was at home where she
> was trying to protect the mom, like "we'll fight him together" type
> thing? So then the only way she knew how to operate was
> through violence. So it was like talking to her about other ways
> to deal with situations when you get escalated, how to deal with
> your anger. I said, "Because this is okay, to be angry. I would be
> angry too if somebody was beating the hell out of my mom, and
> I had to, you know, see that." And that's how they kinda dealt in
> their family, through violence. So she really didn't know any other
> way of operating or communicating, or dealing with those feelings of
> anger. . . . So we talked about different ways, appropriate ways
> of expressing anger through, you know, either journalizing,
> writing things down, or you know, rap, or you know, whatever—art—
> whatever way she felt she needed to get it out. And she was able
> to kind of receive that. I don't know what she did with that. I've
> never seen her again, because she had been up, I think transferring.

COMMUNITY CONCERN FOR SAFETY AT MCCLYMONDS

Violence at McClymonds also had more serious consequences than suspension. In some cases, fights led to shootings and even death. As early as
1991, the district had taken drastic steps to reduce violence on campuses
throughout Oakland. In November 1991, the Board adopted a districtwide
dress code which would ban "expensive jewelry, shorts, and jogging suits."
OUSD board member Toni Cook, who initiated dress code policy, believed
that it would help to reduce crime on and around campuses as well as
reduce rival gang tension at certain school sites (Cutler, 1991). The policy
caught the attention of several critics who viewed it as a possible viola-
tion of students' civil rights. The school district's attorney indicated that
the policy could have serious implementation problems.

The district's earlier efforts to reduce violence on campuses had little
impact. In 1992, school safety was again a major concern for both administrators and parents. During a board meeting in May 1992, board members discussed ways to curtail violence in West Oakland schools (Mahoney,
1992). They listened to testimonies of teachers and other school administrators who had been harassed or threatened by students and nonstudents, who would often hang out at the school. One teacher told about
drunken teenagers walking into her classroom and threatening her and
several students. Board members entertained proposals to strictly enforce
the dress codes and require student badges so that school officials could
know immediately which students belonged on campus. Other board
members argued that mandatory metal detectors be placed on targeted
campuses. Much of the concern for safety followed recent student violence
and the confiscation of weapons from students throughout the district.

Violence had become a very real threat to both teachers and students
at McClymonds. Events at the school that had once reinforced school spirit
and unity had become unsafe territory. Fights and shootings at school
dances and football games often required the police to intervene. Two
McClymonds students commented on the violence:

> We don't feel safe. We call Myrtle Street, the street near our
> school, Murder Street because of all the killings that's happened
> over here.

> That's a place that we stay away from at nighttime. And I used to
> ride my bike all the time, past Myrtle Street, you know, all
> through West Oakland. And because I felt safe to do so, but now,
> we don't feel safe. I mean I [don't] feel comfortable sitting in a
> car near my school toward the nighttime, and you know, we've

been in the car, and we'll go near there, and you know, I would say "Let's go," or someone else would say, "Let's get away from here," because we don't feel safe. You know, she [a shooting victim] didn't do anything that [would cause] anyone to be killed, and that just showed us that it could happen to any of us. And we don't know what's going on, we don't know why they're doing it, but we believe that we were—I mean more of us have been talking about funerals now. We think about our funerals a lot, and we've talked about it, like, "I wonder how many people will come to my funeral," because it's becoming our reality, and something that's so close to home to us that we believe it can happen to any of us, any day.

For some students at "Mac," violence had taken its toll on their lives. The loss of classmates, the inability to concentrate on academics, and the constant paranoia forced some students to look elsewhere for their education. A policy adopted by the school board in 1978 allowed for students in West Oakland to transfer to other schools throughout the district including McClymond's higher performing counterparts Skyline High School and Oakland High School. By the 1991–92 school year, "Mac's" enrollment was down to 562, the lowest in nearly 10 years. Mr. C., a long-time teacher at the school, commented:

Back then, our school was large. We had about 1,000, 1,100 people. Now we're down to about 500. And I think it's been a brain drain in West Oakland. See, what happens is that all the good kids who come out of junior high, their teacher or their counselor recommends that they go to Skyline, or Bishop O'Dowd, or Berkeley High. "Don't go to McClymonds. Because of the environment. Well, the teachers are good down there, but the environment." And I say, well, have 'em come here so they can change the environment. And I can understand that, because the environment is kinda tough, because you have—what happens is with the brain drain, I call it— this is the same thing happening in the community.

District figures estimate that nearly 12 percent of West Oakland high school students attend schools outside of their immediate neighborhood (OUSD Department of Research and Evaluation, 1996b). As Mr. C. speculated, many of the students who choose to attend another high school are the students who have parents active in their child's academic performance. When students transfer to other high schools, it removes both students and parents who would otherwise provide support to McClymonds.

CLOSING MCCLYMONDS HIGH SCHOOL

By the 1991–92 school year, a rumor began to circulate among West Oakland residents that all the problems at McClymonds prompted the school
board to consider closing the school and redirecting the students to other
local high schools. For more than a decade discussions regarding the future
of McClymonds High School included the possibility of closing the school,
the only high school in West Oakland. Numerous fights, low attendance,
high dropout rates, and high suspension rates, had made the school a prime
target for closure. The 1994 McClymonds WASC/CDE report read:

> McClymonds has been plagued with many inner-city social and economic
> ills. As a result, 80 percent of McClymonds students scored below the 50th
> percentile on recent CTBS tests. Most of the school's population read below
> grade level, and suspension rate of students reached 41.9 percent during the
> 1991–1992 academic year. The above statistics prompted the McClymonds
> community and the school Board of Education to propose radical changes
> in the organizational structure, curriculum, and teaching practices in order
> to improve student outcome. (Oakland Unified School District, 1994)

Aside from McClymonds's low performance, there were other reasons for speculation about closing the school. First, the continued low attendance was the result of more and more students transferring to higher
performing schools in the district. Second, there had been plans to redevelop targeted areas of West Oakland that could have impacted the de-
mographic profile of the school. In fact, between 1990 and 1994, 1,359
housing units were demolished in the Acorn housing projects, again displacing hundreds of families (OCCUR, 1990; Coalition for West Oakland
Revitalization, 1994). District projections indicated that the removal of
these units would further reduce the enrollment at McClymonds High
School. Third, the West Oakland community was becoming more attractive to middle- and upper-income nonblack families. The community's
ideal location near downtown Oakland and only 15 minutes from San
Francisco has prompted more middle-income families to purchase property in West Oakland. The unique, large Victorian-style homes coupled
with affordability, has made West Oakland very vulnerable to revitalization, or gentrification. There was speculation that if West Oakland became
more gentrified, these families would likely send their children to other
high schools in the city.

Taking these factors together, some believed that the district was pro-
jecting that, at some point in the future, the school would need to close
for the mere fact that there would simply not be enough students. The
former principal of McClymonds agreed:

My sense at that time was that the district was looking at the low
enrollment. Also, I understand, the building up of West Oakland,
the downtown area, and prime property around McClymonds. The
whites were beginning to move back in. So all of that played into
us hearing that we're going to close McClymonds. Revitalization,
and you know, downtown Oakland. The alumni association was
very vocal. You know, "We need McClymonds. This is the only
high school in West Oakland. What's going to happen to our kids?
Where are they going?"

The board denied that there were any specific plans to close the school
but commented that McClymonds presented serious concerns and that
something would need to be done. While the community had no specific
plan for what they wanted from the district, they were clear that they
wanted West Oakland's only high school to remain open. For the surrounding community, "Mac" was more than just a school. Many parents and
residents of the community had attended the school during its "golden
years" and for them the school represented a community institution. It is
not uncommon for a family to have several generations of children who
attended McClymonds. Additionally, because "Mac" was the only high
school in West Oakland, it represented one of the few places where residents had some sense of community control.

Finally. the community's suspicion was confirmed. After much discussion, the board proposed to close the school and reroute the students
to other schools. In a memo to the board of education, OUSD superintendent Richard P. Mesa outlined the major concerns that had been raised
about the academic productivity of the school. They were the following:

1. Declining test scores
2. High dropout rate
3. Declining enrollment
4. Increase in the number of McClymonds students who seek a transfer to another high school
5. Perceived lack of resources and support from the district
      (Oakland Unified School District Office of the Superintendent,
                                                      March 23, 1992)

The school's principal along with other community groups and representatives organized and lobbied the district to keep the school open.
Dorothy Spann-Agee, who had been the principal at the school for a number of years, had developed strong ties within the surrounding community. The community had also learned that Spann-Agee might be removed

from her post at McClymonds for disagreeing with a powerful school board member. Taken together, these issues further galvanized the community toward saving the school.

During 1989 the school board decided to keep the school open provided that substantial changes were made to the school's overall structure and curriculum. Prior to the school board's threat to close the school, the principal at McClymonds had been contacted by a community organization called BUFFER (Black United Front for Educational Reform) regarding the school's poor academic performance. The group, known for their forceful tactics, confronted the principal and questioned her commitment to educating black children. They wanted to improve the school but needed to know if the principal was going to be an ally in their efforts. A past BUFFER member recalled the confrontation:

> We went to Dr. Agee, who was the principal at the time, and we confronted her in a very hostile manner, you know. We wanted to know what the hell she was doing here, a black woman having gone through these American public schools yourself, and having gone through colleges and universities, and knowing what's required of these kids and that was gonna be required of these kids, and you sitting here as principal of this school, permitting this thing to go on. So then at that point, I mean naturally she felt cornered because she didn't want us to go public with the thing [poor performance at school], so she decided then that she would come here, to meet with us, you know, off the record, you know. Dr. Oba T'Shaka, who is the head of the Black Studies Department of San Francisco State, and myself, and Dr. Agee. Dr. T'Shaka and myself were cochairs of this organization, the Black United Front for Education Reform. We didn't want to put Dr. Agee out there at first, we wanted to have some kind of dialogue with her because it wasn't our intent to hurt her, or do anything of the sort, you know, to do anything that was damaging to her personally. We wanted to make sure that our children [were being served] you know, that it be understood that we get firsthand from her why this thing was happening like this, you know. . . . Well, anyway we came in and we met for some hour and a half here, and she then agreed to bring us certain documents and things there to show.

The meeting between the principal and BUFFER highlighted several key points regarding the school's present condition and its future outlook.

First, the students at the school performed disproportionately lower on virtually all academic measures and indicators. Second, the school provided little academic support and few courses needed for entry into a 4-year college in California. Third, students were being expelled and suspended from the school at alarming rates, which contributed to low enrollment. Fourth, the school lacked basic materials, supplies, and equipment that higher performing schools had, such as computers and chemistry laboratories. Fifth, the surrounding community had become removed from the school with virtually no parent or community involvement.

After the meeting, the principal decided to join BUFFER and assist them in their efforts to improve the school. She provided them with all the documentation they needed to build a case against the district that demanded that they support a project that would "transform" the school. Shortly thereafter, she was removed from her post at McClymonds leaving the school without direct leadership and without support for BUFFER's plan to improve the school.

Reforming McClymonds is perhaps best understood when viewed against the backdrop of Oakland's economic and political challenges. In the 2-year period between 1985 and 1987, Oakland Public Schools struggled to address public concerns regarding accountability due to district-wide corruption, as well as build faith among community members that the fiscal crisis would not jeopardize educational quality. Two factors played a significant role in shaping the structure of opportunity for improving McClymonds high school. First, the Guthrie report in 1985 exposed the district's educational and fiscal problems, which placed the OSUD school board under close public scrutiny. Second, the statewide fiscal crisis required that Oakland Public Schools make deep budgetary cuts that also galvanized community support to keep McClymonds off the chopping block. While these factors galvanized community support, they also encouraged community groups to develop a new educational vision for McClymonds High School.

FIVE

Plans to Transform McClymonds High School

THE INITIATIVE TO TRANSFORM MCCLYMONDS HIGH SCHOOL CAME on the heels of the well-documented Guthrie report that outlined 18 major areas of failure within the Oakland Public School District. Low academic performance, high dropout rates, pervasive mismanagement of funds, and an ongoing battle with the teachers union made the district vulnerable to community pressure to take drastic measures to improve the schools in the city. Working with the principal at McClymonds High School, a small grassroots community organization located in West Oakland began to document the educational inequalities at the school. They found gross neglect on the part of the school district to provide the necessary materials, support, and equipment to McClymonds. Their analysis of the situation was based on the premise that public schools by design were set up to maintain a permanent black underclass. Oscar Wright, one of the West Oakland residents, commented:

> I've been a resident of Oakland for over 40 years. And I've had three children go through the Oakland Public Schools. I found it necessary [to believe], having experienced myself the inequities in education as provided by the public schools for black kids, that a dual system has been set up by the government to make sure that black kids were never given the constitutional commitments of equality, justice, and equal access, whereby perpetuating the permanent underclass of black people. Prior to the formation of BUFFER (Black United Front for Educational Reform), I served as the chairman of the education committee of the Oakland branch of the NAACP. That committee's function was to keep our organization abreast of the educational activities in the public schools in Oakland, as it relates to keeping black kids, or bringing black kids into the mainstream of public education.

Many concerned parents and community members shared the belief that public education was designed to reproduce social inequality. While Wright's comments have conspiratorial undercurrents, his concerns about how systems of education sustain a permanent underclass have been widely theorized (Bourdieu, 1977; Bowles & Gintis, 1976; MacLeod, 1985). Understanding how poverty and social class are mediated through schooling is probably most clearly articulated in the social reproduction literature. The general argument within this literature is that in a class society of ruling elite and dominated groups, there is constant competition for economic power. Access to this economic power is translated through cultural norms that are defined by the ruling class. These cultural norms are transmitted through systems, such as schooling, and reproduce the ruling class economic advantage over oppressed groups.

Wright's comments identify important assumptions about the educational process and therefore particular strategies about how to improve learning for African American students. One important assumption was that to challenge systemic educational problems, African American students need strong advocates to change policy and curriculum in schools.

BEHIND THE EFFORT TO TRANSFORM MCCLYMONDS HIGH

In early 1987 Wright and others formed a network of small grassroots organizations and named it the Black United Front for Educational Reform (BUFFER). BUFFER was started in part from a racial incident that occurred at a nearby junior high school. Wright explained what happened:

> A black student at the school, who happened to be Muslim, was verbally abused by his teacher, who frequently hurled racial slurs at her students. After the student confronted the teacher about her verbal abuse, he was suspended from the school. Shortly thereafter, his mother contacted the Oakland branch of the NAACP and filed several complaints attempting to get her son back into school.

At the time, Oscar Wright was the chairman of the NAACP Education Committee and began to investigate both sides of the story. After talking to the school principal and the student's teachers, he concluded that the school had no grounds to suspend the student. According to Wright, the student was placed back in the school only to realize that he would be subjected to even more abuse and ridicule from other teachers.

Oscar Wright commented about his response to learning about the continued abuse the student faced:

> We had successfully readmitted this young man back into his school. After returning to school, he began to be targeted and harassed. They [teachers] tried to get him into situations where they could be justified in suspending him. When his mother realized what was going on, she came back to us again for help. So I assembled a cross section of black individuals, groups, and organizations. Some of these groups included Pan-Africans, Muslims, and NAACP people. After we came together, we really challenged the school district by picketing at the school to make sure that this teacher was removed, and to force the district to eradicate that kind of treatment for black kids. We thought we were successful in having the teacher removed from the school. But we realized afterward that the district had only given her a paid leave of absence.

ORGANIZING BUFFER FOR ACTION

BUFFER consisted of a coalition of several small grassroots organizations. Their mission was to promote equality, justice, and equal access in education for black children in Oakland. The organization was comprised of a cross section of Oakland's black working-class community. Parents, community activists, church members, and clergy challenged both individual schools and the school district to provide a more equitable education for Oakland's black students. The organization worked to gather documentation that demonstrated that OUSD, by design, tracked black students into low-performance classes. BUFFER had sponsored numerous community meetings, workshops, and conferences to raise the awareness of the pervasive educational inequality in Oakland Public Schools. Wright commented:

> We organized this group in order to promote equality, justice, and equal educational access for Black children. We wanted our children to be educationally competitive. . . . We informed Black parents and the community about their educational rights and their responsibilities. After our initial meeting, we started taking more drastic action against the school district. We picketed; we had press conferences; we demonstrated at the school. Eventually we received verbal commitments from the district about how they

would improve learning opportunities for black kids. Unfortunately, not much happened with their promises.

Many of the issues that BUFFER addressed revolved around school suspensions, expulsions, and general low academic performance in schools where black students were the majority. They found numerous cases where black students had been removed from school for behavior for which they could have stayed enrolled. Reviewing district's documents and attending disciplinary hearings, BUFFER sought to influence district policy regarding suspensions and expulsions, particularly because the existing policy disproportionately affected black students. For example, in 1987 BUFFER began to build a case where they could show that the district, by design, was ill-equipped to educate black students. Another former BUFFER member recalled:

> We were building documentation to show that, by design, the
> school district was tracking black kids into "low-skill" courses. We
> had numerous workshops about the tracking process. Eventually,
> we filed a lawsuit; we testified before the board; we protested and
> picketed; we even testified before a grand jury. We also had
> numerous meetings with principals, just about every major church,
> preacher, and representative in the city.

By the latter part of 1987, the group became even more organized and began to file class action lawsuits on behalf of the citizens of Oakland. By 1988, the organization had a clear understanding of the educational problems facing African American students in Oakland. BUFFER's platform was to provide equal access to educational opportunities for black children in Oakland.

BUFFER's Plan to Improve the School

During the fall of 1989, BUFFER representatives met with the superintendent of Oakland Unified School District to discuss the unequal resources that existed for McClymonds High School compared with other high schools in Oakland. With information gathered from their previous meeting with principal Dorothy Spann-Agee, BUFFER's leadership disclosed information about deteriorating facilities, inferior curriculum and materials, and general lack of concern on the part of the school district.

BUFFER was concerned with McClymonds High's failure to provide students with Advanced Placement (AP) courses, college preparatory science, and other issues regarding educational inequality. BUFFER's concerns were threefold: (1) academic performance, (2) educational equity in school and district policy, and (3) equal opportunity and access to higher education. BUFFER's demands included more college preparation courses, better materials and curriculum, a review of suspension policy, and an improvement of school facilities. For example, McClymonds High offered no college preparation courses in chemistry, physics, or biology because they lacked the facilities and materials. Also, although records indicated that their students utilized a computer laboratory, the school had no computer lab nor did it have plans to implement one. BUFFER's president discussed this situation:

> The school was supposed to have, according to the records, a certain number of computers for students to use. They also had three science classes with one set of science books for all the students in the course! That means that those students were not able to take those books home because the books had to stay at the school. Now how can a high school student do homework without a book? Also the school had no chemistry lab, no wet lab with sinks, and things like that.

BUFFER's goal was to address the issue of educational inequality at McClymonds High by increasing the number of college preparation courses, providing computers and technical assistance, and providing new text books to all of McClymonds' students. Their demands of the district involved the immediate and direct improvement of school facilities, curriculum, and instruction. They had diagnosed and articulated the problem at the school as a willful neglect on the part of the district to provide resources and support to the school. They indicted the superintendent and the school board for failing to provide resources to the school.

In the past, BUFFER had pressured the Oakland school board to make improvements in the curriculum, materials, and facilities at other schools. From past experience and knowledge of BUFFER's sometimes radical tactics, the superintendent also was aware of the type of pressure BUFFER could exert on the school board. The superintendent urged BUFFER to take these demands to the board of education in a public forum because he was not in the position to initiate those changes. In January 1988, superintendent Joe Coto suggested that a task force be assembled to further investigate the possibility of designing and implementing a plan to improve the school.

The task force was comprised of both original BUFFER members from the community and newly recruited professionals. The task force was given the responsibility to refine the proposed plan and develop strategies for implementing the proposed changes at McClymonds. As a strategy, BUFFER members knew that, after they presented their concerns to the board, they would be asked to draft a plan to address the issues that they raised.

BUFFER's New Expert Members

Preempting the board's request to develop a plan, BUFFER invited several African American professors, educators, and attorneys to assist them with the development of a plan to improve the school. Inviting educational experts and professionals was a strategic move to establish more credibility and to attract professionals who could support the organization's efforts. From 1987 to 1990 BUFFER's membership grew from 30 to as many as 125. BUFFER was successful in recruiting a highly educated group of professionals who were professors, educational administrators, doctors, and lawyers. In a relatively short time BUFFER had become a visible and viable organization in Oakland. By 1989 BUFFER had a created a diverse membership with both professional and blue-collar membership. A past BUFFER member recalled, "We were able to bring in a lot of scholars and professors with Ph.D.'s. We had doctors, we had lawyers, we had the educators, we had carpenters, and we just had all kinds of people, custodians, and everything, as active members of the organization."

The recruitment of new members for the organization was a strategic move to solidify its already wide community support and to exploit the credibility of credentialed experts in the area of education. Having members who were lawyers and professors added more credibility to the organization's original platform, which was to demonstrate the district's willful neglect of black children. The new members also were instrumental in the development of a plan that would be used to implement the changes BUFFER had demanded. In early 1989 BUFFER representatives began drafting a plan that spelled out the problems that confronted McClymonds and advocated for drastic changes in the curriculum and other aspects of the school. While there was no specific discussion for how these changes would take place, it did charge the school board with the responsibility of supporting the community's efforts to reform the school. While the plan was well received and approved "in concept" by the school board, no action was taken for nearly 2 years. Numerous changes in administration both at the school site and within the district prevented the plan from getting implemented. From 1988 until 1992, the school had been through a number of changes. The school had had four principals; there had been a high turnover of staff, the district administration who had supported the initiative changed; and there had been three different superintendents.

Consequently, the plan was reviewed in 1989 but was never formally adopted by the board and implemented. Additionally, in the process of drafting a proposal to the school board, ideological divisions emerged within BUFFER's membership regarding the plan's specific content. While all of its members shared the same ideology about the need to improve the conditions for black students at McClymonds High School, they could not agree about the best way to improve academic performance. For some, the best way to improve the school was by addressing the concrete issues that had been raised prior to the recruitment of the new members. The founding members advocated better textbooks, access to computers, and the inclusion of college preparation course. However, BUFFER's newer members defined the problem in very different terms. Their concern was that the school lacked a cultural inclusion of African identity. Some of the new members wanted to address educational inequality at McClymonds High by implementing an African-centered curriculum that would also utilize computers, new textbooks, and college preparation courses.

BUFFER had debated before about what they wanted for African American students at the school, but these discussions had never included a discussion about Afrocentric education. BUFFER's original intent was to address the immediate problems that contributed to the school's low performance. The newer members, however, advocated building student's identity through an Afrocentric curriculum. One BUFFER respondent indicated that the new "experts" needed to explain and teach the membership about Afrocentrism.

> I explained my position to them. I said, when you talk about Afrocentrism, what exactly do you mean? They explained that it was about the history of Africa and Egypt and all that kind of stuff. They talked about all these African principles and it was like some type of philosophy.

BUFFER's main concern was that black students receive an equal quality education, which tangentially involved the integration of black history. The primary concern for BUFFER had been to provide African American students with the tools necessary for them to compete with their white counterparts. This involved a sophisticated understanding of admission requirements, college preparation courses, and access to precollege curriculum—not necessarily Afrocentrism. The president indicated:

I understood that the state, the federal government, and the school district had already written the rules required for graduation, college admission, and so on. The rules said that in order to be able to enter into college you've got to have so many units of mathematics, and they specify the different subjects within mathematics. Now if you don't have these you're not going anywhere. That's what I was interested in.

While the "experts" felt that these curriculum requirements were necessary, they also indicated that merely concentrating on college preparation was insufficient because it lacked a cultural identity. The critique from the newer members was that providing the same educational opportunities as higher performing white schools did not go far enough to challenge the damaging content of what was actually being taught—which was, as some members put it, white supremacy. The founding members of the organization held their position and advocated that the plan needed to provide students with the same educational opportunities (i.e., college prep courses, better facilities, and better curriculum) as students at higher performing schools.

The Experts' Plan to Improve the School

A few of the scholars who joined or were associated with BUFFER's efforts (Oba T'Shaka, Wade Nobles, Asa Hilliard) had been well known in the African American educational community as proponents of African-centered education. In 1990 the movement to utilize an Afrocentric framework in urban schools had blossomed in several urban school districts across the country including Washington, D.C., Baltimore, Milwaukee, New York, and Detroit. Some of the same scholars that were influential in promoting Afrocentric education across the country had become key members of BUFFER's leadership. Some had published books, others had centers that focused on Afrocentric research, and most of them had access to resources (i.e., research, funding sources, institutional name recognition) available at their respective universities. Most of the new BUFFER members were college graduates and many held advanced degrees. Some of them were lawyers, professors, company executives, and medical doctors. Mr. F., an attorney who had joined BUFFER, commented:

The founding BUFFER members basically said, "Let's just take the best educational system out of a white community and give it to blacks." They assumed that this would bring about educational equality. They did not consider the cultural needs of the black students. In fact, there had been no assessment of the cultural needs of the students in that community. I believe that a school that is 90 percent African American has drastically different cultural needs than a school that is 90 percent white. It's a mistake to assume that both schools have the same needs. I urged the members to consider the racial and cultural needs of black students.

Eventually some of the new members assumed leadership roles in the organization, which gave them more leverage among BUFFER's membership in advocating for an Afrocentric program. In most cases, the "experts" had been recruited for their knowledge and understanding of issues confronting African American students. Consequently, it wasn't difficult to convince other members for the need of Afrocentric education—after all the "experts" knew what was best. Mr. F., who had joined the effort to develop the plan, was also responsible for investigating the district's legal responsibility to provide McClymonds with resources to implement BUFFER's plan. His comments reflect a clear articulation and diagnosis of the problems from the point of view of the "experts."

Basically, the idea was to sue the school district for purposeful miseducation because the school district knew at the beginning of the school year that a large portion of African Americans students would fail. Yet the state mandated that all students go through the educational process anyway, fully aware that the institution itself was not going to provide the educational experience that would meet their needs. So, since you mandate students to go through an educational process for 12 years, it was my belief that the schools should be responsible for teaching something that's relevant so that they can actually make it in the society.

So I began some research and found the Educational Code provision 51-204, Section 51, 204 of the Education Code, which says any course of study must be designed to meet the needs of the students. Now that was a bombshell. Education Code 51-204 says any course of study must be designed to meet the needs of the students. This blew my mind. I said, "That's it!" That is what we could build our case and educational struggle on. We needed to show that current educational strategies in Oakland did not meet African American students' academic needs.

We filed a class action lawsuit against the Oakland Unified School District on behalf of all African American students and their parents. There were about 90,000 people represented in the lawsuit. The lawsuit sued for purposeful miseducation of black students and stated that the educational system created low self-esteem and low self-worth among black students. This is contrary to the Educational Code. While students were required to attend school by law, we showed that doing so, under current conditions, also injured them because the schools only celebrated and promoted white culture. We believed that students were entitled to an education that benefited them, that was designed to meet their needs. The language from that Code section was quoted throughout the lawsuit. The remedy was not a bunch of money. We argued that the district be required to hire a team of experts who would design an educational program that would meet the needs of the students.

Mr. F.'s comments here reflected the ideological framework of BUFFER's newer "experts." This ideology forwarded the position that McClymonds students, among other black students in Oakland, suffered from a damaged self-esteem brought on by an educational system that exclusively promoted and celebrated European culture. In fact, other newer members expressed that student failure among African Americans could be attributed to a curriculum and pedagogy that was based on European ideology and was in conflict with how black students live and learn. This viewpoint was reflected again in minutes from a board meeting where Wade Nobles was asked to present progress on the plan. He commented:

McClymonds has decayed and has become a place of educational failure. Children learn best and achieve their maximum when the learning environment reflects and respects their image and their interests. The way children thrive is when they see their own image and interests in the proposition.

Wade Nobles had published numerous articles and books and was well known for his work with African American boys. The Hawk Federation, the name of his "manhood training" project, received national attention for being a model for working with young black males. Nobles was also a vocal advocate for Afrocentric ways of educating black children. He was also the director of San Francisco State University's Center for Applied Studies in Educational Achievement and the head of the Oakland-based black think tank, Institute for the Advanced Study of Black Family and Culture. Nobles believed that by using ancient Kemitic or Egyptian philosophy, black teenage males could excel academically and become leaders in their community. His Afrocentric approach is based on the belief that "while everyone can be taught the same information, they cannot learn it in the same ways because of differing cultural experiences" (C. Jackson, 1991, p. 3). Nobles commented that "in our (African) tradition, the whole process of education was not compartmentalized as in Western culture. There was not school work, then church work, then house work. All learning was interconnected."

The Hawk project was the result of research conducted by Nobles and students at San Francisco State University and had received wide support among black educators throughout the country. It was natural then that Nobles was involved with the project particularly because he was also a West Oakland resident. As such, Nobles brought with him a great deal of notoriety, influence, and prestige to the McClymonds project.

On Becoming Afrocentric

Other "expert" members of BUFFER were influenced by the Afrocentric movement while in college or while pursuing their graduate degrees. Some members had grown up in neighborhoods similar to West Oakland and had survived and "made it out" because they were positively impacted by an Afrocentric teacher or course in high school or college. Based on some of their own positive experiences with learning about black identity, these members testified about the powerful impact an Afrocentric education could have on black children. Mr. F. admitted to having a nationalist bias in his legal work because he had come under the influence of the Afrocentric movement in college. In fact, he credits black studies and black history for bringing him out of self-destructive behavior when he was in high school:

> I first got involved with the black liberation struggle during my senior year in high school. . . . In my earlier years as a juvenile, I was involved with crime, drugs, and violence. I was really into the lifestyle that leads to the penitentiary or the graveyard. I was OK with where I was heading until two things happened.
>
> When I turned 18 in December 1977, I went to jail for a little minor incident. I was doing first-degree burglaries and robberies and all kinds of stuff. Then I got caught, as an adult, and went through the court system. I just realized that everyone being locked up was black and poor and that the prosecutors, judges, and district attorneys were almost all white. That really disturbed me seeing the judge sentence us black poor folks all day long.
>
> When I went back to school the next semester, I was blessed to get into a couple of classes. One was a black history class,

which I had never taken before. There were so many things that I simply didn't know. The TV special *Roots* came out around that time. Watching *Roots* and reading about all this black history was really enlightening to me. I literally was spellbound, and for the first time was paying attention in my classes. . . . I had never read or known any of that history. That class began to encourage me to read and study for the first time.

While not all the "experts" in BUFFER shared the same experience presented here, they did share the idea that Afrocentric education could transform and improve the students' lives at McClymonds. The Afrocentric movement had profoundly influenced Mr. F. In his view, the material that he read and the concepts that he learned, saved him from the streets. Mr. F. viewed his life as being very similar to students at McClymonds High in West Oakland. For him, if they were exposed to the same material and information that he had been provided, such an experience would motivate them to learn and excel in school. Personal testimonies such as Mr. F.'s story allowed other members to see the connections between Afrocentric education and academic excellence, which in turn made the idea of Afrocentric education much more appealing. After considerable debate, BUFFER decided that a combination of both Afrocentric curriculum and traditional academic support and programming for college entrance was desirable. Oscar Wright recalled:

I just wanted to make sure that black kids' education was comparable to others. There were people like Dr. Wade Nobles, and people like Dr. T'Shaka, and other professors who were very involved in black studies and African things. They suggested that we call it an Afrocentric program. I had no knowledge of what that meant because I had never heard of that term before. I'm 73 now, and I had never heard that term. But when they talked about it, it made sense to me, because they were very active members and were part of the leadership here in BUFFER. So you know, naturally, I did not oppose this idea.

Many of the original BUFFER members were unfamiliar with the term *Afrocentric* and needed further clarification and information about what the "experts" meant when they referred to McClymonds as an Afrocentric school. The experts had conducted several workshops and had convened discussion groups in order to educate members of BUFFER who had little knowledge of Afrocentrism. These discussions included handouts, articles from periodicals, and books that argued for the necessity of Afrocentric education. Still, some BUFFER members disagreed with an Afrocentric approach. One member reflected on how he felt about the proposal to make McClymonds an Afrocentric school:

> That wasn't my philosophy. I wanted [black history] to be infused into the curriculum. For example, a science instructor might say, "I want you to give me a report on George Washington Carver's contributions to science." But that wasn't quite consistent with what they [Oba T'Shaka, Wade Nobles] wanted. They wanted a special type of teaching from Africa. They wanted to focus on Egypt or Ethiopia. They wanted to talk about African history and things like that which is good, but it had nothing to do with the fact that students had to satisfy graduation and college entrance requirements.

The central item of contention was whether or not Africa and African themes and philosophy should be the central force in designing the curriculum. While most agreed that black history and African contributions was needed and should be included within the proposal, the "experts" believed that African precepts, axioms, philosophy, and themes should guide, direct, and inform the content of the proposed changes. For other members, these items were merely peripheral to the need to engage students in higher order learning, critical thinking, and more college preparation. After much discussion, the "experts" were successful in convincing the other members to draft a plan where Afrocentric education would be central.

THE FINAL PLAN TO TRANSFORM MCCLYMONDS HIGH

Shortly thereafter, Wade Nobles was named the principal investigator of the project and was granted full authority on the behalf of BUFFER to draft a final proposal for the new program. In 1992 the Area assistant superintendent Dennis Chanonas and superintendent Richard Mesa received a proposal from Wade Nobles (1992) that they believed demonstrated potential for improving the school. The proposal, entitled The McClymonds International Science, Culture, and Technology High School Project: The Project to Make McClymonds High School a School of Excellence, outlined the objectives and goals of the project, and described its overall mission as follows:

> To make McClymonds High School a place where children will receive the best education that Oakland had to offer, Educational Excellence at the new

McClymonds will be centered in and be guided by African/African American educational philosophy and teacher techniques that produced black men and women of achievement and greatness in this country and the world. (Nobles, 1992, p. 5)

The goal and objective of the project was to "reopen McClymonds High School as a model African-Centered Educational Institution whose focus is 'educational excellence' in Science, Culture, and Technology in a pluralist American society and multicultural world" (Nobles, 1992, p. 5). Specifically, the project was designed to

1. Adopt/refine where appropriate and invent/create where necessary, culturally consistent (African-centered) curriculum materials, subject areas, teaching technologies, and site-management policies, procedures, and practices
2. Plan, design, and conduct a culturally consistent (African-centered) teacher-training institute for the McClymonds faculty and staff
3. Plan, design, and conduct a culturally consistent (African-centered) staff development and site-administration training
4. Establish necessary advisory/governing boards (parents, business, educators, and so on) to monitor and hold the project accountable to the best interests of West Oakland's children and families
5. Conduct community forums/meetings designed to inform and educate interested parties and the community at-large about the expectations, requirements, and benefits of the McClymonds International Science, Culture, and Technology High School

The plan was to reopen McClymonds in September 1992 as a model African-Centered Educational Institution that would focus on educational excellence in science, culture, and technology. The proposal called for dramatic modifications in the "entire educational process" and called for radical reform in teaching, curriculum, and assessment. With a site-based management team of parents, the revitalization project was designed, implemented, and managed by the Center for Applied Cultural Studies and Educational Achievement. The project was also jointly sponsored by the Educational Research and Development Center, the State Department of Education, and California State University at San Francisco. Under the direction of Wade Nobles, the proposal laid out a 5-year plan which included state-mandated curriculum guidelines.

The project was governed by a team of parents, teachers, staff, students, and experts and advocated for full independence and noninterference from the school board. The proposal stated that "shared decision-making, interdependence in authority to govern, and full independence . . . along with a covenant of noninterference . . . will provide the necessary conditions for guaranteeing the creation of 'educational excellence'" (Nobles, 1992, p. 7). The educational focus spelled out seven African-centered precepts that guided the overall philosophy of the school.

> With African-centered education, the task of educating African American children will be guided by the understanding and utilization of African-centered cultural precepts to stimulate and reinforce "educational excellence" and the attainment of maximum achievement in every aspect of education. They are:
>
> 1. Every child not only can learn but can learn everything.
> 2. Optimal or maximum learning takes place when knowledge, knowing, and the knower are culturally connected. Effective teaching and learning will be characterized by cooperation and mutuality.
> 3. The value of individual achievement is internalized when achievement is related to one's ability to contribute to the well-being and welfare of one's self, family, and community.
> 4. Every aspect of schooling is coordinated and intentionally designed to guide each student to the next higher level of performance/functioning and mastery.
> 5. The educational experience is intentionally orchestrated to provide and reinforce in the students an attitude, ability, and willingness to contribute to their own, as well as others', human fulfillment.
> 6. The total educational process is demonstrably linked to the student's and the community's well-being and welfare.
> 7. Each aspect or part of the educational process complements every other aspect of the process and, in so doing, result in greater educational reinforcement and attainment.
>
> (p. 4)

The proposal defined *African-centered* as a concept that categorizes "a quality of thought and practice which is rooted in the cultural image and interests of people of African ancestry and which represents and reflects the life experiences, history, and traditions of people of African ancestry as the center of analyses" (Nobles, 1992, p. 1). In regard to education, the terms *Afrocentric* or *African-centered* convey the notion that African cultural precepts, processes, laws, and experiences guide students toward academic excellence. Nobles conveyed this idea in the proposal:

> African-centered multicultural education is driven by truth, respect for knowledge, desire to learn, and a passion for excellence. In regard to "centric" education, the importance of culture is not simply relegated or mini-

mized to the task of being sensitive to cultural differences or superficially appreciating or exploring the common ground of different people. As the foundation for multicultural education, culture as both the process and the subject of education, will serve as the medium and mechanism for teaching, learning, counseling, and educational management/administration. (p. 3)

Over the next several months Nobles and Richard Mesa discussed items in the proposal that Mesa felt needed clarification. While Mesa supported the intent of the proposal, he was skeptical about the proposal's content, as he expressed in a March 23, 1992, memo to the school board:

Recently, Area Assistant Superintendent Dennis Chaconas and I received a proposal from Dr. Wade Nobles that we both felt had some intriguing possibilities, but at the same time raised a number of questions and concerns. Since our initial meeting, Dr. Nobles's and I have had a number of discussions to clarify the questions and to respond to my concerns. What I originally thought were problems have been easily resolved because of Dr. Nobles's openness and because we basically agreed to a great extent on what the reforms for a school like McClymonds should be. (Oakland Unified School District Office of the Superintendent, March 23, 1992, p. 1)

The subsequent meetings between Mesa and Nobles addressed several concerns Mesa had with the content of the proposal. Mesa wanted to assure that the program would not alienate other nonblack students at the school. He was also concerned that using the term Afrocentric would create a situation where students would be given an image of what it meant to be black and therefore dismiss each student's unique experience and understanding of blackness. Mesa indicated this in his memo to the board of education:

I was concerned that ethnocentric curriculum would focus only on the history and culture of one group and that history and culture would be interpreted in a narrow way to which students would have to be indoctrinated. My concern grew out of the fact that, in the past, this has occurred among minorities to the end that too often the definition of what it is to be black, brown, Asian, or any other ethnic or cultural group has been defined by a group that sets itself up as the arbitrary determiners of cultural identity. . . . No student should be made to feel more or less black, more or less brown, or Asian, because of what that individual finally chooses to form his identity. . . . We agree that one ethnic or racial group shall not be enhanced through the denigration of another. My discussions with Dr. Nobles have assured me that this is not his intent. Nevertheless, I feel that he and I will need to work closely together to make sure that no misunderstandings develop in this area.

While Mesa held these specific reservations about the project, his primary concern was that students would be presented with a static model of racial identity—one that may not have included the life experiences of many of McClymonds students. How would biracial students understand and relate to the material? Would it alienate all nonblack students? How relevant would the Afrocentric material be to the students given the fact that many of the students came from low-income families? Having previous experience working with racial politics within schools, Mesa was well aware of the potential hazards that could arise when other groups are left out of the curriculum. On one hand, Mesa supported the proposal, yet on the other hand, he was cautious about the potential fallout from other racial groups in the city. For example, he was concerned that it could be perceived that blacks have their own school, which could then lead to quasi racially segregated schools. Mesa stated:

> Dr. Nobles and I still have some issues to discuss and resolve. To begin with, there are some concepts and terms used in the proposal that I do not fully understand the implications of for students. Some of these are the following: The scientific and moral criteria that African Americans should use to authenticate reality—I am not sure how constraining to students' choices this concept may be. I believe with him that people have the right to center themselves in their own cultures, but I do not agree that it is their "responsibility" to do so. We need to discuss further what is meant by "culturally consistent" for the same reasons indicated above. However, what I really believe Dr. Nobles means, although we have not discussed it, is that what he seeks, and I agree with, is to try to get not only African Americans but other students to return to the traditional values that have helped black people, and others not only to survive, but to achieve cultural greatness. . . . My caveat is that, as much as we might want our children or students to follow those precepts, in American democratic schools we cannot coerce or indoctrinate them to do so.

While Mesa had the responsibility to allow the community to define for itself the type of education they wanted for their children, he also needed to assure that such an education was fair and inclusive of all students. Even though McClymond's student body was primarily African American, he was compelled to consider the rights of those who were nonblack. Thus, while he supported the plan in theory, he paid close attention to the process and content that was to be implemented. Mesa indicated: "While the initial emphasis may be ethnocentric, in this case Afrocentric, students must be moved to a culturally inclusive orientation that makes all students, respective of race and ethnicity, feel part of the school and the educational program" (p. 2).

As such, Nobles assured Mesa that the intent of the project was not to exclude students but rather to acknowledge cultural differences and use culture as the basis for educational transformation. In the proposal, Nobles (1992) articulated this point:

> The nature of the African-centered educational process, in fact, encourages and demands that the varied and diverse sociocultural precepts, traditions, and histories of the total student population be reflected throughout the system of knowledge, teaching, and learning. In effect, the universality of Afrocentric education will serve as the key to achieving true multiculturalism and diversity. (p. 2)

After several meetings, Nobles had addressed many of Mesa's initial concerns about the project. They both agreed that in addition to employing cultural strategies, the plan would also pursue several other objectives:

1. A tutoring program for 10 percent of the students at McClymonds
2. Interactive instruction
3. Development of the core curriculum
4. Attention to the students' life circumstances in general
5. Medical examination of all students in the first 2 years
6. Assistance and involvement with parents in a broad comprehensive way
7. Attention to making the school climate one that makes all students feel valued, accepted, safe, and secure

On March 23, 1992, Richard Mesa forwarded his comments, which included both his reservations and support of various items, to the board of education. Included with his comments was the revised proposal that Nobles and his team had prepared. During the board meeting 2 days later, McClymonds PTA chairperson Frank Allen, Oscar Wright, and several other key players in the project testified before the board about the need for the board to adopt the proposal for McClymonds and to hire Wade Nobles as the consultant who would implement the project. Nobles testified before the school board:

> Madam Chair, Superintendent Mesa, and Directors of the Board, please allow me to express my appreciation and excitement for the opportunity to address you tonight. Many of you know that as a professional psychologist and educator, I have provided staff development and teacher in-service training at McClymonds, Oakland High School, and Martin Luther King Elementary and serve on several educational boards, commissions, and cabinets.
>
> However, the McClymonds project is personal to me. I believe in public education. I am a product of Oakland Public Schools. I graduated from Oakland High School. All my children and my granddaughter have [attended] or are attending a public school in Oakland. I live in West Oakland. My second son graduated from McClymonds. I have a host of nieces [and] nephews who have attended and graduated from McClymonds. My great-nephew is the starting center for the McClymonds football team. This project is personal for me because I do live in West Oakland. West Oakland is my community, and McClymonds is my community's high school. I want, therefore, to offer the skills, expertise, and resources under my command to help make McClymonds the best school in the nation.

His testimony continued by advocating that McClymonds be opened the following year as a demonstration school. Along with outlining some of the problems that he believed plagued the school, Nobles also presented an explanation and justification for using Afrocentric education at McClymonds. After presenting the eight principals, he explained to them in more detail the meaning of African-centered education. He stated, "The McClymonds transformation process will, in effect, make the education of African American equal to educational excellence by"

1. Recreating the learning environment
2. Retraining teachers and staff in new teaching techniques
3. Adopting high-level curriculum standards and educational materials
4. Requiring new expectations of excellence for teachers and students
5. Utilizing an African-centered educational process that respects and reflects the best of African American education
6. Adopting the educational "intent" of reproducing and refining the best of the African/African American genius and ethnical traits

Mesa recommended adopting the proposal in concept and working out the specifics at a later date. Director Anderson motioned to approve the plan and was seconded by Director Lawson. During the evening of March 25, 1992, the plan was approved unanimously by every member of the board. Under the command of Wade Nobles, McClymonds would reopen the following year as a demonstration school with a focus on Afrocentric education.

Six

Implementing the Afrocentric Program

AFTER RECEIVING APPROVAL, NOBLES AND HIS TEAM WORKED ON revising the proposal and designing the actual implementation of the project. Nobles' team consisted of renowned educators, scholars, Afrocentric theorists, teachers, and residents, all who assisted with the design of the implementation process. The new focus would concentrate on educational excellence in science, culture, and technology by creating an environment where the entire educational process reflected African-centered principles, culture, and values. The goal of the initiative was to use African-centered educational strategies in curriculum content, pedagogies, and outcome assessment. The courses were to be consistent with the University of California's "A through F" course requirements as well as the latest cutting edge educational materials and technology.

TRANSFORMING THE SCHOOL

On June 18, 1992, Nobles entered into a contract with the school district that outlined the responsibilities for the first year of the project. The school district had allocated $349,800 toward the project with an additional $71,000 for a secretary, office supplies and equipment, duplication costs, and travel, totaling $420,000 (Oakland Unified School District, 1992). The first year of the 4-year project was dedicated to designing the program to assure that its curriculum content was consistent with the California curriculum framework for instruction and the curriculum guidelines for the Oakland Unified School District and to develop a culturally relevant educational curriculum. The project would begin with ninth-graders, and each consecutive year, the project would review and revise the entire curriculum for the next grade level (Gilmore, 1996).

The faculty at McClymonds had the opportunity to visit successful Afrocentric programs in Atlanta, Chicago, and Detroit as a means of facilitating a smoother transition for the school. During these site visits, teachers from McClymonds received feedback about how to refine their own teaching and curriculum by other Afrocentric teachers. The project used existing teachers from McClymonds rather than recruiting teachers who had already demonstrated a proficiency in Afrocentric teaching. During the first year of the program, the teachers and administration participated in several in-service workshops that introduced the basic ideas of Afrocentric philosophy and practice. These workshops were presented by leading experts in the field of Afrocentric theory. Upon completion of their review of the school's curriculum, the team of experts determined that the teachers at the school needed to become more familiar with the Afrocentric method of instruction (Gilmore, 1996). The experts made a compelling argument that the success of the project would be hinged upon the ability of the teachers and administrators to integrate African-centered philosophy into their everyday practices both in and outside of the classroom.

One of the key components of the new program was integrating the eight cultural precepts and adopting an ancient Egyptian code of conduct or values system called Ma'at. The system or code was used as a way to change the culture of the school from one of disunity and disorder to one of unity and harmony. The Principles of Ma'at define the personal, social, moral, ethical, political, spiritual, and economical principles students should follow (Nobles, 1996). The principles are as follows:

1. *Truth*: One must speak truth and do truth.
2. *Justice* is seen as a persona: social, economic, and political "rightness" embedded in the balance between individual liberty and societal expectations.
3. *Righteousness* is seen as governing or relating, which is driven by the principle of reciprocity.
4. *Propriety* acknowledges that the most fundamental human desires are happiness and affection.
5. *Balance* refers to the state wherein all the elements are in equilibrium.
6. *Harmony* acknowledges the importance of order, balance, rhythm, and rapport for the sense of homeostasis.
7. *Order* is considered the first virtue because nothing is possible without order, including good.

These principles and others were to become the school's credo and were integrated into various lessons and school activities and rituals. These concepts were officially adopted by the school and posted in classrooms and throughout the hallways. Tina Gilmore (1996) commented:

The goal of the African-Centered Transformation Program at McClymonds was to wholeheartedly incorporate the Eight Cultural Precepts, Principles of Ma'at, and the Alasal Tarey (Project Driven Education) into the school philosophy, so that the staff could function as efficient and competent educators of McClymonds' children. The new philosophy, the resulting credo, and the drive to officially create an African-centered curriculum resulted in a new manual that outlined the guidelines for teaching, instruction, and practice at McClymonds. Curriculum-wise, a few new required courses were added to supplement the already existing sequence of courses, and African-oriented rituals were put into place. (pp. 63–64)

These principles were to form the core of all curriculum, pedagogical and assessment changes at the school. These principles were to inform new courses, rules, and behavioral conduct for students, teachers, and staff.

THE NEW CURRICULUM

Changes in the curriculum were not as dramatic as what had been proposed. Some of the new courses merely enhanced the existing curriculum. During the first year of the program, two new courses were added for freshmen— one was titled "Introduction to Science, Culture, and Technology," the other was titled "Introduction to African American Studies." There was one important change to the graduation requirements that required all students to take core courses, all of which exceeded the University of California A–F course sequence requirement. Each student must have completed a total of 270 units in order to graduate and must have maintained at least a 2.0 grade point average. In order to provide an Afrocentric foundation for learning, all entering 9th-grade students were required to enroll in core courses (i.e., math, science, Introduction to African American Studies, English) with academic specialization beginning in the 10th grade. McClymonds graduates also were required to complete 100 hours of community service and 80 hours of school service, in addition to passing the required district proficiency tests (Nobles, 1995). Gilmore (1996) commented:

> The major differences between the old and new curriculum are the additional new courses in Science, Culture, Technology, and African-American Studies, as well as the addition of African Dance and other electives. Students are also required to take two extra courses in science, math, and history in order to exceed the A–F requirements. (Gilmore, 1996, p. 66)

The changes in the curriculum and graduation requirements reflected a desire on the part of the experts to "raise the standards" for students at

McClymonds. This was accomplished in part because the proposal had committed to exceeding the district's curriculum framework; but also the experts who had made the changes wanted to push teachers and students to raise their expectations about what could be accomplished at the school. Table 6.1 illustrates how teachers allocated classroom time to prepare students for various educational projects.

The new curriculum also encouraged teachers to place an emphasis on incorporating African and African American precepts such as veneration of ancestors, communalism, and collectivism to inspire learning. The role of the teacher is to make the curriculum come alive by translating information, experiences and meaning so that students might apply it to their own environment. The project supported teachers in developing course materials in order to carry out these goals. For example, several science teachers at the school developed a syllabus that linked the technical information about the biological sciences with the Afrocentric principles of Ma'at based on truth, balance, harmony, order, propriety, justice, and reciprocity (see Table 6.2).

Similarly, one of the school's math teachers used key Afrocentric concepts to enhance sections of her basic algebra course. For example, in the lesson where students learn about the Pythagorean theorem, students were

Table 6.1. McClymonds High School International Science Culture and Technology Alasal-Tarey (Project-Driven Education)

Common Lesson Plan Design	
Opening of the Moment	5 mins.
State Goals, Objectives, Student Outcomes	7 mins.
Review Previous Day's Lesson—Bridge	5 mins.
Learning Dialogs	53 mins.
Teacher-directed instruction	
Reading, writing	
Interactive learning, group discussion	
Student-directed instruction	
Student interaction	
Homework Assignments and Follow-up	5 mins.
Wrap-up, Clarification, and Questions	10 mins.
Closure	2 mins.
Total Classroom Time	87 mins.

Table 6.2. McClymonds Afrocentric Biology Curriculum

Week	Ma'at Principle	Biological Concepts
Week 1	Truth	Learning about truth through scientific evidence and reason
Week 2	Balance	Understanding cell equilibrium and functions
Week 3	Harmony	Understanding transportation through cell wall and surrounding environment of the cell
Week 4	Order	Understanding basic cell structure
Week 5	Propriety	Understanding the proper function of a healthy cell (discuss viruses, cancer, steroids)
Week 6	Justice	Understanding the proper environment for cells to grow
Week 7	Righteousness	Understanding how cells try to self-correct from an imbalance or outside influence

asked to demonstrate and discuss how ancient Kemetic people applied the Pythagorean theorem in their civilization. Students were also given vocabulary words for the lesson that were written on the board. This particular classroom was decorated with posters such as "Great Queens of Africa" and "Models of Success." The teacher explained the assignment and invited them to interact in the discussion while she recorded their responses on a graph on the chalkboard. Most of the students seemed to be engaged in the assignment and were actively participating.

TEACHERS' PERSPECTIVE: TUMULTUOUS TIMES

The beginning of the 1992 school year was tumultuous for McClymonds. First, the new principal was not given his assignment until 2 weeks before the start of the school year and had little knowledge about the new project that had been planned for the school. Second, the district had recently replaced the school's administration with all new personnel. Third, a high staff-turnover rate forced the district to hire a significant number of substitute teachers to teach certain classes, reducing the number of credentialed teachers at the school. In fact, there were five substitutes who were hired on long-term contracts. Fourth, by November the teachers union had gone on a 5-week strike leaving the school with virtually no stable faculty.

By the time the strike had ended, the faculty and staff at the school had struggled to come together as a unit. New faculty and long-term substitutes who were unfamiliar with the students and the West Oakland community perhaps had the most difficult time during the year. By the time they were introduced to the Afrocentric project, many of the teachers were suspicious of any program that was supported by the district. For some teachers, the project was seen as another move by the board of education to assuage the community's concern about the school's past poor performance. Others, however, viewed the project as a real opportunity to take control of the school and finally be a part of something that could potentially improve both the image of the school and the academic performance of the students. One teacher commented that "there was little consensus among us about whether we supported it or not, some of us did, some of us didn't. Those that didn't support it tended to just stay out of the way and not get involved."

The inability of the faculty to gain consensus was due in part because many of the faculty members were new and had little investment in the school or the students. Additionally, the project could not hire new Afrocentric-proficient teachers for the project. As a result, many teachers had to do additional reading and attend seminars outside of their regular teaching workload in order to become more familiar with Afrocentric education. This created some immediate challenges for the project. First, teachers who did not support the project were still "required" to adopt the new Afrocentric philosophy, framework, and pedagogy. This meant that even if they voiced concerns about the project, they would still be "encouraged" to adopt it in their teaching materials and pedagogy. For some teachers this meant that in reality, they would use the Afrocentric material when they believed it to be convenient and appropriate. Mr. C. had been a teacher at McClymonds for nearly 30 years. He had taught generations of students and their families and recognized a need for an Afrocentric curriculum at the school. As a supporter of the project, Mr. C. shared a number of problems with the project:

> The project had problems to begin with because we didn't have the right teachers. We should have closed down the school entirely and conducted in-service training after everyone was more prepared. There were a lot of inherent problems with the process. The people in administration weren't really sold on the program. Can you imagine having someone who is in charge of the program but not sold on it? Dr. Noble often used the expression, "We're building the plane while we're flying it." The commitment simply wasn't there from all the teachers.

The phrase that Nobles frequently used, "we are building a plane while we are flying it," referred to the risky and experimental nature of the project. While many of the teachers supported the project in theory, they experienced great difficulty in using the project's material in practice. The program required that the teachers not only alter the content of what they taught, but it also challenged some of their basic assumptions about their own pedagogy. The teachers were required to attend in-service training and numerous workshops that provided them with a wealth of information about Afrocentric concepts but very little about how to use it in their classrooms. Concepts such as synergy, collectivism, and egalitarianism all were concepts the teachers adopted as the Afrocentric credo, but for many of them it was unclear what these terms actually looked like in the classroom. The principal recalled:

> Some of the teachers supported it, some didn't. Mostly, they wanted Wade's team to come in and show them what Afrocentric teaching looked like with some real techniques and lessons. For example, I was a math teacher, and I used to go and train other math teachers. I would say, "Ok, here is how we can show students how to add and subtract fractions." I would go and actually show them, you know, step-by-step. That is what some of the teachers wanted from Wade, but they never got it. He refused to go into the classroom. They asked for this numerous times. But you see, Wade is not a high school teacher and this was a real big problem, because he couldn't show them how to use these concepts in the classroom.

Many of the trainers were themselves Afrocentric scholars and theorists who had little knowledge about what actually happens in a high school classroom. Because they lacked knowledge about teaching practices, the teachers were left guessing about how to use the material in the classroom. As a result, they wanted to see Nobles himself go into a classroom and teach his own ideas on Afrocentrism. The gap between theory and practice was made evident in one teacher's comment that "we needed to see him [Nobles] go and try to teach this stuff to our students. I understood the theory part about the need for culturally consistent education. But it just didn't work; we needed to see some successful examples of what he wanted us to do." Gilmore (1996) noted both teacher confusion and student reactions in her observations:

> At the African-centered in-service meetings, many of the new teachers expressed their desire to understand the Transformation Project. Toward the

end of the school year, many of the same teachers claim to be fully impervi-
ous to the expectations of the Afrocentric guidelines. In the meantime, their
students are the ones who suffer the effects of their limited knowledge of
Afrocentricity. On one occasion, I had the opportunity to speak with a group
of students while substituting for a French teacher. When I asked them what
they thought of the Afrocentric program, I was told that the program was
only present at McClymonds in theory, and that they had yet to learn of any
Afrocentric agenda in any of their classes. (p. 104)

Additionally, teachers were given readings to review in order to assist them with their classroom teaching. While some teachers took the
opportunity to read and review the materials, others viewed the request
as an additional burden on their already full workload. Moreover, some
teachers voiced concerns about the presence of other racial groups at the
school. They felt that focusing entirely on African Americans could alienate the voices and experiences of the growing Latino, Vietnamese, and
Laotian population at the school. One teacher indicated:

> Some of the teachers here had real problems with the focus on
> Africa because of the presence of other cultures in the school. We
> also had to do a lot of work outside of school, like going to
> lectures, reading all these books; it was a lot of extra work. Some
> of the teachers felt threatened by all this.

No Buy-In

For Mr. C., the project never was designed to really help the students at
McClymonds. He felt that it was yet another attempt for the board to address a serious problem by "washing their hands" of the responsibility to
address the problems at the school. His discussion points to what he believed to be the motivation behind the district's support of the project:

> My feeling is that school districts take on funding projects because
> it brings a little more money into the doors. The district gave lip
> service to the project. They thought we could put a dashiki on, say
> a few words, and that would be it. They really didn't buy into the
> complete concept of an African-centered person. Some of the
> district leadership just said, "Well, let's just throw some money at it
> and see what happens." I don't think people really believed in it; I
> think people just said, "Oh, we'll give it a shot," expecting the
> project to fail. When the project falls apart, they can respond by
> saying, "Well, we gave it a shot. We gave you money, we let you

try it." I mean that's like giving a Band-Aid to someone who's got a deep gash that's spewing out blood and saying, "Okay, I gave you a Band-Aid, why didn't you stop the bleeding?" Or giving someone with cancer disinfectant and hoping they'll get better. It just doesn't work like that. I don't think that the support was ever really there— it was more lip service.

Mr. C.'s comments reflect the concerns of someone who supported the effort. He pointed to the way in which the district interpreted the problem at McClymonds and questioned their commitment to addressing the problem. In his view, the district's financial support did not represent an actual commitment to solving the problem at the school. Rather it was one way the district could appear as if they were attempting to improve the school without actual engagement. For Mr. C. and others, the board viewed the school as being in such a desperate condition that they were willing to try anything. Thus, on one hand, if the project was successful the board could appear as supportive and committed to improving the school. On the other hand, if the project failed, they could place blame elsewhere because they had "given the community their chance."

For Mr. C., the Afrocentric program was one way of addressing the problems the school faced. In fact, Mr. C. identified himself as an Afrocentric person, meaning that what he was trying to do in his classroom was also reflected in his life choices. For him, an Afrocentric teacher needed to go beyond merely "using" Afrocentric education, but rather it needed to be an integral part of their worldview. He commented:

I was always an African-centered person. I think in order to effectively teach from an African-centered perspective, you must live from that perspective. That doesn't mean that I can't teach European history, or a European can't teach African history. It just means teaching from your heart. But many of the teachers simply did not teach from that perspective, it was just window dressing, colorful activities, and rituals.

For Mr. C., Afrocentric education needed to go beyond techniques and teaching styles and needed to become "a way of life." Because this failed to happen, he viewed the program as mere window dressing that didn't go far enough to address the needs of the students. While there were varying degrees of support for the project among the faculty, there was some agreement about the implementation process of the project as a whole. First, there was a gap between Afrocentric theory and practice. While Afrocentric education made perfectly good sense to the teachers, they were unclear about how to implement it in their classrooms. Second, high turn-over among administration and staff, coupled with the decision to use the existing teachers at the school rather than to hire new ones, fragmented any potential unified support for the project.

Additionally, Mr. C. made an interesting observation. His comments about the district wanting to "just throw some money at the problem" points to the degree to which the board of education was committed to actually improving the school. For him, the allocation of funds for the project was merely an effort to shift responsibility and blame back into the hands of the community. Thus he believed that while they provided mone-tary support, there was no commitment on the board's part to support the transformation project. This was due to the fact that the district again re-moved the principal from McClymonds in 1994, along with other key administrative staff, and yielded to the teachers union request not to trans-fer teachers who didn't support the project.

COMMUNITY'S PERSPECTIVE: HOW MUCH DOES IT COST?

After Wade Nobles signed the initial contract, the community began to question the amount of money that was given to the project and how that money was to be spent. The initial contract allocated $420,000 to Wade Nobles's Center for Applied Cultural Studies and Educational Achievement for the first year of the project (Oakland Unified School District, 1992). Among the most controversial items in the budget were personnel costs at $118,000, and consultants costing $150,000. The personnel costs in-cluded only two positions: Project Director and Administrative Assistant. These two staff positions alone were over 30 percent of the entire budget for the first year. In both private and public conversations, Nobles tried to assure members of the community that the outcomes of the project would justify the costs. In a public community forum, several community resi-dents asked Nobles to justify his own $90,000 salary* (Peeks, 1995). With trepidation, Nobles assured them that the money would be well spent and that there would be dramatic improvements in the school. In fact, it was

---

*It was clear that this issue was a difficult one to discuss for some of the informants. In fact, while some informants acknowledged their concern about how the money was spent, when I asked them to talk more about it, they were hesitant. In one instance, the inter-viewee began to discuss this issue and then abruptly ended by saying that "I'd really rather not get in to all that, it's not important." I attributed this to the fact that Nobles is well respected in the black community. The apprehension in discussing this issue was an effort not to divert attention away from the issues they believed were more pertinent to the story, therefore avoiding an unnecessary "airing of dirty laundry."

stated in the proposal, "Even though evidence of improvement will be immediate, the achievement of McClymonds transformation, obviously, is going to require a long-term commitment as well as full and complete allocation of the resources" (Nobles, 1992, p. 7). For Nobles and his team, the outcomes would justify the cost of the project. The proposal outlined several outcomes the project was to produce:

> While improvement on the standard state mandated-measures of achievement should be evidenced in the first year, the real indicators of success will be the establishment of effective educational leadership at McClymonds; a passion for learning amongst the students, teachers, and parents; better behavioral and ethical conduct; a collective vision and commitment to educational excellence; and a dedication and loyalty to the McClymonds transformation process. (Nobles, 1992, p. 7)

Many community residents were dissatisfied with Nobles' response, which further fueled rumors about the cost of the project and the actual work that was to be conducted. One of the largest expenditures in the budget was allocated for other consultants to assist with the project. These consultants were hired as trainers and guest speakers for a lecture series designed to further educate students, teachers, and parents about Afrocentric education. These consultants had been well known for their work in developing Afrocentric theory. Many were college professors and/or researchers who had contributed to the formation of the Afrocentric movement.

Nommo Lectures

Named after the African concept of *Nommo*, which means creative power through word, the project included a series of lectures from internationally renowned Afrocentric activists, artists, and scholars titled the Distinguished Nommo Lectures Series. Among them were Asa G. Hilliard, Leonard Jeffries, Na´im Akbar, Sonia Sanchez, Sister Souljah, John Henrik Clark, Molefi Kete Asante, LaFrancis Rodgers-Rose, Hunter Adams III, Brother Nuradeen, Vulindlela Wobogo, Jacob Carruthers, Ivan Van Sertima, Benjamin Chavis, and Marimba Ani. Held in the school auditorium on Friday afternoons and Saturday mornings six times during the year, these lectures were open to the teachers, parents, and students of the West Oakland community. The purpose of the lectures was to stimulate, create, and reinforce educational excellence and the attainment of maximum educational achievement for all children attending McClymonds High and to activate the creative power of knowledge and critical thinking of the West Oakland community (Cotton, 1995). The project was created by the

1993 senior class officers as a class project that was aimed at demonstrating a commitment to their community and educational excellence. Gilmore (1996) noted her observations of several Nommo lectures:

> The Distinguished Nommo Lectures are characterized by a traditional libation and inspirational thought before the lecture. The ceremony begins as the faculty, administration, and guest speakers enter the auditorium for the processional. While drummers play an African beat, teachers, most of them dressed in traditional African clothing and Kenté cloth, walk down the center aisle to the front of the auditorium and take their seats on stage in front rows. The audience participates by clapping to the beat of the drums. Once everyone is seated, the host begins the libation. During this time thanks is given to the elders and the ancestors, after which water is poured into the pot of a tree. Before the guest speaker is introduced, the school's dance troupe performs an African dance to the rhythm of the drum beat. Following the performance, the senior class officers present an award of merit to the Distinguished Nommo Lecturer, who accepts the award and presents the speech. (pp. 69–70)

Though the senior class sponsored the project, community residents, local students, and parents rarely attended these lectures. While the surrounding community was invited, they were skeptical about the usefulness of what was being presented. Many of them were also unaware of the lectures and expressed little interest in learning about Afrocentrism. Many of those who attended the lectures were members of a growing Afrocentric community in the Bay Area. In the audience were black bookstore owners, African craft venders, college students, and local black scholars from nearby universities all of whom were familiar with many of the featured Afrocentric scholars. The Afrocentric community came from places other than West Oakland such as Vallejo, Sacramento, San Francisco, and San Jose. One West Oakland community resident who was active in the process commented:

> I would have liked everybody to have attended those lectures, especially the people in the neighborhood. They [neighborhood people] just didn't come. I guess they did not understand the purpose of the effort. We tried to get the word out and educate them more about the issues. Parents just seemed to feel like their children should just go to school and learn whatever the school has to teach them. They don't know or care about what their children learn. So we had to deal with that barrier. There were a lot of educators, but there weren't really many West Oakland community people. Teachers, professors, lawyers know from good jobs and professions. Some of the people on my block seemed

not to really care to get involved. They were working hard trying to make ends meet, trying to make it everyday.

The difficulty in getting parents and other surrounding residents involved was complicated by the fact that the school had very little parental involvement to begin with. Because many of the school's parents were poor and working-class, concerns about finding child care and taking off from work made attending these lectures even less attractive. Additionally, most of them were unfamiliar with the featured guest speakers and had little knowledge about Afrocentric education. Another resident recalled:

> There was limited community involvement even though they were behind it in spirit. Those of us who were active in the community were tired of seeing our children getting low grades, not achieving, not graduating, dropping out of school, not getting into college. We wanted to address these issues so that our children would have a fair chance to succeed.

Similar to the concerns expressed by the teachers, many community residents were also skeptical about the project from the onset. Several community residents had expressed concern about the administration's failure to keep the school safe and provide students with the necessary materials. They wanted to see how the Afrocentric project would accomplish the following:

1. Reduce the number of fights
2. Reduce the number of suspensions
3. Increase academic performance
4. Provide higher quality materials and academic support

Nobles and his team addressed these concerns in several community forums and continued to move forward with the project. The tentative community involvement contributed the idea that it was not a community project. Thus, while the community was aware of the program, they never took ownership of it. In other words, it was largely seen as a "Wade Nobles" project and its focus on Afrocentrism alienated many community residents.

FROM THE STUDENTS' PERSPECTIVE

During the first year of the program, many of the students were oblivious to the changes in their new school. With the exception of a new

course on African history and a new Swahili course, many students were
unaware of the Afrocentric project. From time to time students would
comment about the program but few actually recognized the changes at
the school. Some students recognized the new murals, posters, and African proverbs in the hallways but really had no idea that they were now
attending an "Afrocentric" school. It wasn't until the school began to hold
assemblies and promote the new Afrocentric classes that students took
notice of the changes at the school. On Fridays, students and teachers
were encouraged to wear African clothing to promote Afrocentric awareness. One of the students at McClymonds commented about her reflections about the project:

> Students saw it both ways. Some of the students were saying, "It
> was a bunch of junk, because we're not really learning anything
> new. They just putting on funny-looking hats and all those colors
> just to show us that we are all African, or whatever." And then
> some students' views were like, "It was really helpful." Some of
> the students got into it. For example, we had an African ball.
> And in my ninth grade year, we had African history classes,
> where we basically learned everything about Egypt and about
> Africa. That's the only class that I can really say tied in the
> entire Afrocentric curriculum. My other classes, they tried to tie
> it in. Like my geometry class, he made an attempt to try to have
> the principles of Ma´at and implemented the ideas in like some
> of the material, but it just didn't work, so we just basically
> learned regular geometry.

When the students realized that there had been Afrocentric changes
at their school, some were skeptical about how learning about Africa would
help improve the school. For some, the program became a point of ridicule because, while they understood that they were learning African languages, dance, and rituals, the focus on African culture was irrelevant to
their everyday lives. Moreover, they experienced the frustration of trying
to figure out how and why teachers were using the curriculum in their
various classes. The same student recalled:

> My geometry teacher would say something like, "Based upon the
> principles of Ma´at, we're going to practice the African concept of
> Balance." He would try to use a math problem as an example and
> show how it balances out to illustrate the principle. We would
> also learn about Imhotep, and discuss how he was the father of
> medicine and mathematics. The African material was more helpful

for subjects like history, but the other classes, like math, it wasn't really helpful.

Additionally, the everyday experience of violence, poverty, teen pregnancy, and drug use were realities that never were addressed in the program. Students had expressed the need to have the material make more sense to them in ways they could use in their everyday lives. A counselor at the school explained:

> They [Nobles' team] weren't dealing with the students' issues, they were trying to get the students to think about Africa, you know wearing Kenté cloth and all that, but the students would say things like "what the hell does this have to do with me?" The effort didn't validate their experience on the streets. I feel that the kids need to know about our culture, but I think in order to be able to understand it some of their more basic needs like eating and safety need to be in place. Our students are really into survival and when they hear about the kings of Egypt they ask themselves how is that information going to make things better for them. I think that students needed more concrete connections about how African culture would help them. They [Nobles' team] did not consider that, they just came in to show our students how to be a real black African kid and how to be better at being black.

The counselor pointed out several interesting assumptions that were made about working with students from McClymonds. The first assumption was that the students' experiences inside the school were more important than their experiences outside of school. In other words, the changes in the curriculum content as well as the school environment would contribute to higher performing, well-behaved, and engaged students. This approach, as the counselor has pointed out, ignored the everyday realities of the students. Much of their lives were spent outside of school, and, as a result, school was only a small part of their entire educational experience. The second assumption was that African culture, worldview, rituals, or philosophy was sufficient in addressing the needs of the students. She commented about what students would say about the project: "'What's all this African shit? This old mumbo jumbo.' That's how they responded to some of the material and activities. They would say, 'What's that shit got to do with me making some money?' You know, that type of thing." While the counselor acknowledged the importance that these things have in contributing to a healthier esteem, she also recognized the importance of addressing the immediate needs, issues, and problems confronting the students.

"Howz It Gonna Help Me Make Some Money?"

By focusing only on African culture, the project largely ignored the fact that many of the students had families who received AFDC, or they did not live with their parents, or they had to work to help pay for rent. A student commented about the day-to-day struggles she faced outside of school and how economic challenges make school even more difficult.

> I'm seventeen years old, I have a 5-month-old daughter, my boyfriend's in jail, and I live with my father and my stepmother who don't support me and my child, you know what I'm saying? I'm like stuck in this situation. I love my daughter to death and I got to give her what she wants and what she needs, but it's just not happening the way I want it to. I got a job that doesn't pay me enough to take care of my baby and myself! If she doesn't have any milk or if she doesn't have any diapers, what am I suppose to do? I have a lot to think about, you know. I have go to school, I have go to work, or I have pick up my baby, and I got bills to pay. Sometimes I want to go to the movies, but I can't because I don't have any money. I don't have any child care support, you know everything is coming at me all at the same time you know you! Sometimes I feel just feel like fuck it! Why try, I ain't going to school, for what!

These challenges present formidable barriers to academic success. Students' lives outside of school have a profound impact on what happens inside of school. The stress of making ends meet is often difficult for adults, but for youth the challenges are sometimes even more demanding. Balancing her school activities and raising her child, all while working, makes support critical not simply for academic success but also for survival. Fortunately, with support from a counselor at the school, this student was able to get the support she needed to navigate her way through school and raising her child. McClymond's students overwhelmingly expressed a need for more counselors, and for programs and curriculum that were more pertinent to their everyday lives. For example, it was important for many of the students to earn money so that they could contribute to the family by helping to pay rent or buy food and clothing. This was particularly important considering that there were few opportunities for viable jobs for youth in the West Oakland community. Because of the dearth of jobs in the community, students are often resourceful in finding ways to earn money; both legal and illegal. Two students at the school articulated this idea:

> I've tried to get a job, but nobody wants to hire me. I need money but I can't get a job, so what am I suppose to do? My momma doesn't have the money, my girlfriend doesn't have the money, nobody you know has the money, but I got to live. So what are my options but to steal money or sell drugs. If you got two rocks right here in your pocket, you can sell it, well that's an easy twenty dollars.

Similarly, another student commented:

> You know, basically what they call most of the things that they do in West Oakland is "getting your hustle on." Meaning doing whatever you can to get what you need. Some people do hair, other people I know do nails or baby-sitting. There are a selected few that got jobs, but for those who don't, drug selling and prostitution are the biggest, biggest money makers.

Another student commented when asked what do they do after school to earn money:

> You do whatever you can do to get money. It's usually nothing positive. You know what I mean? I know people, you know, that have tried to get jobs, but it's always you're either too young, or it's just too hard. I've had friends prostitute just because money is just so important to them. I have friends sell drugs, either marijuana or crack cocaine. That's mostly what guys do is sell drugs. The girls are mostly into prostitution of some kind.

Another student commented:

> It's almost like everybody out here has got some kind of hustle that they do on the side. I sell shirts, you know, and make movies and stuff like that. You can't support yourself on most of these jobs, seven dollars and eight dollars an hour. You know, after I help with rent, I have seventy dollars left over at the end of the pay period to pay for bus fare, childcare, and food. Now

seventy dollars has got to last me till the next two weeks, you
know what I'm saying. So, it's like the job situation is just all bad.

From the students' perspective, the ability to work and earn money
was important. Unfortunately, McClymonds did not offer a job placement
program. Nevertheless, some students took advantage of job placement
programs sponsored by the City of Oakland. These jobs included part-time
work usually in nearby downtown Oakland or across town in local retail
stores or fast-food restaurants. Students often commented about how they
would complement income from their part-time jobs by selling T-shirts,
incense, or copied CDs. Not all students at the school participated in part-
time jobs. Some students sought illegal ways to make ends meet during
nonschool hours: selling drugs, burglary, and theft.

While the Afrocentric curriculum attempted to address the problems
at the school, it largely ignored student's activities outside of the school
context. Moreover, because the curriculum didn't address the immediate
concerns of the students nor did it engage them it ways that were meaningful, some students perceived the program as an arrogant attempt to
"teach them what it means to be black."

HOW TO BECOME BETTER AT BEING BLACK

The Afrocentric transformation project at McClymonds began with major
problems both at the district and at the actual school site. With only token
support from the district, the project was expected to have limited success. Changes in the administration and faculty created even greater challenges for the project. In short, Wade Nobles and his staff faced an uphill
battle in several ways. First, Nobles had to convince the board of education that the Afrocentric approach was appropriate for McClymonds. Second, he was required to work with teachers who were not invested in the
success of the school or the students. This was largely because many teachers either were new to the school or would soon be leaving the school.
Third, Nobles had to address concerns from the community about how the
money for the project would be spent and was compelled to justify the
cost of the program. He maintained that the merits of the project justified
its cost. Under scrutiny by teachers, administrators, and by the community, Nobles maintained that an Afrocentric approach would best serve the
students at the school.

The transformation was indeed wrought with problems. While there
was little consensus among teachers about the utility of the project, few

were able to use the material in their classes in ways that were useful and meaningful to the students. The training, seminars, and workshops proved to be futile in the classroom when teachers were confronted with every-day problems. For example, Gilmore (1996) recorded one such observa-tion of teachers at the school during the project:

> There were about 25 students present, 7 of whom came in late. The teacher gave an introductory lecture, in which he tried to relate the day's activity to everything on the planet. This was his attempt to connect the learning pro-cess with the principles of Synergy and Collectivism. Some of the topics he discussed were: "How does this process fit in with my values? Is it OK to work on things that are dead?" The teacher had to work hard to keep noisy stu-dents and those who came in late from interrupting the flow of his lecture. The teacher then began to discuss the "larger" picture, "What connects us all," with the students. He then drew from the principles of Ma´at. "Is it righteous, honorable, or moral?" he asked. "How do the principles of Afrocentrism fit into all of this?" . . . very few of the students were listening. Many were talk-ing among themselves. Though it was clear that the teacher himself had a pretty good understanding of the Afrocentric theories and principles, it wasn't quite clear that the students understood these concepts. (p. 77)

Moreover, students were not engaged largely because they viewed the material as irrelevant to their lives. In fact, some students ridiculed and accused the project of trying to show them how to become a better black person. A school counselor articulated this dilemma quite well:

> But you don't know, so it's like sometimes people come with this thing of really being better than a person, and trying to say, "OK, I'm better than you. I have this knowledge. I'm Afrocentric, and I'm gonna teach you how to be this, and change you, and make you a better person." And I think for the kids it's—you know, it's hard for a lot of adults to receive that, let alone some kids who already are trying to deal with survival issues and stuff like that.

Indeed transforming McClymonds into an "International Afrocentric Academy" proved to be a difficult task for a number of reasons. Rooted in the most fundamental assumption about using an Afrocentric or African-centered approach was that the students at the school would accept, re-spond, and embrace the narrow model of black identity which they were presented. While many concede that the role of ethnic identity and cul-ture in schooling plays an important role in academic performance, one cannot underestimate the ways in which the students' environment comes to influence how student see themselves. At McClymonds, the inability to consider such factors as student poverty, the district's political climate, and the community's interpretation of academic improvement all contributed to a misdiagnosis and treatment of the problems at McClymonds.

FROM EGYPT TO WEST OAKLAND:
OUTCOMES AND EXPECTATIONS

The reform effort at McClymonds was largely aimed at the cultural transformation of students, staff, and the school environment. The overall strategy of the project was to integrate a curriculum that would validate the educational experiences of all students by providing a culturally relevant curriculum that rejected damaging Eurocentric ideas. As stated in the school's strategic plan, "McClymonds will consciously use the best of African American culture, values, traditions, techniques, and precepts to stimulate, create, and reinforce educational excellence and the attainment of maximum educational achievement for all children attending the school" (Nobles & Mann, 1994, p. 6). As demonstrated earlier, the students at the school grappled with class issues brought on by living in an economically deprived community. Their identities were informed by the day-to-day reality of joblessness and lack of resources. The students, teachers, and community residents understood that racial and cultural identity could not be isolated from exigencies of class.

For the students, this was reflected in a lack of interest in Afrocentric materials and curriculum. Put another way, they were unable to make the connections between the contributions of Kemet (Egypt) to the world and the realities of West Oakland. For teachers, this meant that they had to be reeducated and trained in ways that they believed didn't address all of the needs of the students. In addition, even those who supported the project experienced difficulty in making connections between Afrocentric theory and practice. For the surrounding working-class community, the project had little relevance because it didn't address some of their more immediate concerns such as employment, child care, health care, and housing. In short, because the project focused only on racial and cultural identity, it overlooked the ways in which other factors contributed to the formation of students' identities.

SEVEN

The Failure of Afrocentric Reform at McClymonds High School

IN 1995 THE LAST YEAR OF THE PROJECT AT MCCLYMONDS HIGH School began, but unfortunately, the project had contributed little toward improving the school. A new principal was placed at the school, and, while he valued Afrocentric education, his vision of the school placed the program on the periphery. Without a vice-principal to assist him, he was overwhelmed with student issues as well as general administrative duties. As a result, the transformation project was further marginalized at the school.

OUTCOMES: WAS MCCLYMONDS TRANSFORMED?

The project set out to transform McClymonds High with ambitious goals and outcomes. From the onset, BUFFER had outlined a number of items that they demanded be addressed at the school. Based on an extensive review of the school's academic performance, BUFFER had concluded that the following issues should be addressed:

1. More college preparation courses
2. More students taking SAT and advanced placement tests
3. Books and better materials for students
4. Reduction in suspensions and expulsions
5. Higher scoring on standardized testing

After recruiting a number of experts to assist them with developing a plan to improve the school, BUFFER yielded to the influence of the team of experts who amended BUFFER's initial list of issues to also include African-centered curriculum and materials, culturally consistent teacher training and staff development, a community driven governing body, and community forums designed to inform the surrounding community about the new changes at the school.

While not explicitly stated, the new items that were listed in the final proposal were void of any language that identified particular academic outcomes for the school. In fact, the final proposal included no mention of improvement in grade point averages, student attendance rates, or drop-out rates. Thus, while BUFFER's initial concerns for McClymonds were based largely on academic outcomes and performance, the final plan that was developed lacked any strong language about academic indicators that could point to the school's improvement. Table 7.1 presents a list of academic outcome indicators with data for the years covered by the program. The indicators include outcomes that had been a concern of BUFFER.

"We Blew a Golden Opportunity"

It is apparent that by examining the data for these academic indicators that the transformation project fell short of transforming the school. In fact, based on these outcomes, the project had little, if any, impact on the academic performance of the students at the school. One teacher commented about the outcomes of the project: "We blew a golden opportunity. We had a good deal of money and everything, but we let it slip away. The only thing that the project left behind here is this booklet and these affirmations on this poster here in room 213."

Table 7.1. Academic Outcome Indicators During the Transformation Project at McClymonds High School, 1992-1996

Indicator	1992	1993	1994	1995	1996
Enrollment	637	*	676	632	629
GPA College Prep Courses	1.56	1.10	1.55	1.34	1.41
Dropout Rate	11%	14.8%	24.4%	22.2%	22%
Suspension Rate	28%	*	16%	31%	*
Enrolled in C.S.U, U.C., & Peralta Colleges	38	34	20	19	10
Number of Students Taking the SAT	23	38	20	46	37
Number of Graduates	62	83	61	66	63

* Not available.

Source: Oakland Unified School District, Department of Research and Evaluation, 1996a.

This teacher realized that the project had not accomplished all that it had set out to do. In fact, he also was aware that the project was still under scrutiny by some who continued to question the amount of money that was spent on the project. After the initial contract that was signed in 1992 for $420,000, another $290,000 was approved on July 1 of the following year. Community members began to express concerns about Nobles's promise to improve academic performance when after the first 2 years of the project virtually no improvements had been made. A past school board member commented about the board's concern regarding the amount they were spending on the project:

> We felt that we didn't get what we actually paid for; we didn't get our money's worth. I know that we approved, on at least two occasions, a considerable amount of money, something like $300,000 or more each time. I remember that Pete Mesa wasn't entirely excited about the project because he wanted to assure that it would be inclusive of all students.

The board member indicated that for a number of years, they wanted to see something done at McClymonds that could turn the school around. But they really didn't have a clear idea of what they wanted. On July 1, 1995 the board approved another $147,500 toward the project. In all, the board had allocated $857,000 toward the transformation project at the school. The same board member commented that the school had not changed that much although Nobles experienced substantial obstacles. Members of the board of education were not alone in questioning the value of the project. Teachers, community residents, and local educators all knew that nearly a million dollars had been spent on the project and very little had been done to change the school.

WHY DID THE PROJECT FAIL?

The plan to improve McClymonds was ultimately guided solely by the notion that academic performance could be improved by addressing and reclaiming ancient African ideology as a framework for educating African American students. An attorney and member of BUFFER commented:

> We believe that the educational system creates low self-esteem, low self-worth, and injures black students. Students are required to go to school by law, and yet it injures them because it pro-motes white culture, white civilization, and it promotes white

supremacy. There needed to be a remedy for that. [We believed that] the students were entitled to an education that benefited them and that was designed to meet their needs. So from the start, [race] was a relevant and direct issue. When you talk about giving a proper education and relevant education, you had to talk about African history, Afrocentric culture. For example, we had people looking at textbooks and we realized that black folks are not present in many textbooks.

The attorney's analysis was focused on how BUFFER could improve black students' educational experiences by focusing on racial and ethnic issues of representation. Before the educational experts and black middle-class professionals joined BUFFER, original members defined the problem as neglect on the part of the district to provide adequate resources, and advocated for hiring qualified teachers; offering college preparation courses; providing facilities for biology and chemistry laboratories; purchasing books, computers, and software; and providing a safe and clean school. As BUFFER came under the influence of black middle-class professionals who themselves were admittedly committed to improving the conditions for West Oakland's working-class students, the goals and objectives shifted toward Afrocentric solutions. The Afrocentric transformation initiative was ultimately influenced by scholars and other black middle-class professionals who were able to use their research, writing, and analytical skills to reframe BUFFER's original intent, which was to address the school's concrete educational problems. While the new members of BUFFER had well-meaning intentions on improving McClymonds, the emphasis they placed on Afrocentric education diverted valuable resources from what could have been an effort to improve student performance by creating curriculum and programs that met students' needs both inside and outside of school. A more complex view of black youth identity would have considered how social class and economic isolation shapes the way the black youth see themselves and how they perform in school. This view of black youth identity could have also translated to greater student engagement because students make connections with curriculum that they see as relevant to their everyday struggles.

From the outset, however, the Afrocentric project at McClymonds had an uphill battle. One might simply conclude that poor communities have more problems and consequently greater educational challenges. While this may in part be true, there are at least two additional factors that contributed to the demise of the Afrocentric project at McClymonds. First, the project operated from an oversimplified model of youth identity. The challenge for Afrocentric scholars and practitioners is to add more complexity to their understanding of black identity, an understanding that considers issues such as class, sexuality, gender and so on. The second reason the project failed was that black middle-class members of BUFFER developed a reform strategy that did not address some of the more immediate and pressing needs of the school. Because the project focused entirely on strategies that strengthened ethnic identity through African culture, the reform effort at McClymonds did not address the ways in which poverty impacted the needs of the students at the school.

Static View of Race and Identity

Afrocentric educators often design reform strategies with a static view of race and ethnic identity. This idea was evident in another reform effort in Oakland when the Oakland School Board decided in 1998 to adopt Ebonics as an official language (Bazely, 1996a, 1996d; Payton, 1996). In 1995, the Oakland Board of Education formed a task force in order to investigate the academic performance of African American students in the district. For nearly a year, the Task Force on the Education of African American Students worked closely with community leaders, parents, teachers, professors, and educational researchers in order to define and articulate a plan that would improve the language performance of African American students. On December 18, 1996, the task force presented its findings to the board of education:

> There is persuasive, empirical evidence that—predicated on analysis of the phonology, morphology, and syntax that currently exists as systematic, rule-governed, and predictable—patterns exist in the grammar of African American speech. The validated and persuasive linguistic evidence is that African Americans (1) have retained a West and Niger-Congo African linguistic structure in the substratum of their speech and (2) by this criterion are not native speakers of a black dialect or any other dialect of English. Moreover, there is persuasive, empirical evidence that, owing to their history as United States slave descendants of West and Niger-Congo African origin, to the extent that African Americans have been born into, reared in, and continue to live in linguistic environments that are different from the Euro-American English-speaking population, African American people and their children are from home environments in which a language other than the English language is dominant. (Task Force on the Education of African American Students, 1996a)

The Task Force on the Education of African American Students argued that language competencies of African American students in Oakland were influenced by linguistic patterns from West African culture. The main argument the task force put forward was that "African American students speak and bring to school a 'primary home' language that is not standard English, and that their need for specially designed curricula [and] committed, sensitive, highly trained teachers . . . is real and must be addressed" (Task Force on the Education of African American Students, 1996b, p. 2). The task force challenged the board of education to take bold measures to:

1. Recognize African American Language/Ebonics as the primary language of many African American students
2. Add African American Language/Ebonics to all district documents, offering optional placement of students in classes or programs serving limited English proficient students.
3. Provide access to all services, current or planned, for limited-English-proficient students to limited-English African American Language/Ebonics students
   (Task Force on the Education of African American Students, 1996b).

Shortly after the board of education adopted the task force's recommendations, the media spun the story and sold it to the American public as another educational gimmick to garner more resources for black students (Rodgers, 1997). The highly publicized story caught the attention of many educators, policy makers, and parents who viewed the board's decision to make Ebonics an official language as a joke, at best, and irresponsible, at worst. Similar to the Afrocentric project at McClymonds, community members debated what they believed to be best for educating Oakland's African American students (Bazely, 1996b; Payton, 1996; "Welcome to Ebonics II", 1996).

What is key about this debate is that it illustrates how race and class shape school improvement efforts in urban schools. For some blacks in Oakland, Ebonics was viewed as yet another attempt by the district to remedy problems with ephemeral Band-Aid-like solutions. For others, the move signaled a bold and daring move to reclaim black cultural and racial identity in the face of policies that often marginalized black students (Bazely, 1996c; Brand, 1996). The Ebonics resolution did in some ways grapple with how social class and poverty shapes language performance, but again, the resolution placed an overemphasis on how West African culture influences language, while failing to consider how social class might shape linguistic competencies. Mrs. Nia, a long-time language teacher in Oakland, a black woman, and a key player on the task force, commented:

I was a classroom teacher working in a school where students spoke several languages. I worked with large numbers of children who spoke Cantonese, Cambodian, Lao, Me-in, Spanish, Tonga, Tagalog. I noticed that our [black] children had the most difficulty with writing. When I looked at the issue of language, I didn't understand why our [black] children were reluctant to write. I concluded that they don't write because our language is not accepted. It's demeaned, and the culture of our people is not accepted and is placed at a lower status because of white supremacy. Then it was clearer to me why everybody else's kids, even though they didn't speak English, would write and perform better.

Despite the fact that the language groups she was referring to shared similar experiences of racism because they did not speak Standard English, she concluded that other groups tended to outperform black students because they clearly understood that their native language, which was spoken at home, was simply different from English, which was mostly used in school. She and others involved with the Ebonics project believed that if black students could also make the simple distinction between the type of English they spoke at home (Ebonics) and the type they needed to speak at school (Standard English), perhaps they could also improve their standard English competencies. However, she indicated that acquisition of Standard English was also shaped by socioeconomic factors.

We have children who, because of social isolation in the projects, live in home environments where Ebonics is spoken 100 percent of the time. They simply don't hear Standard English at home. They come to school speaking the language that they are familiar with at home. You also have other children who may have learned both languages at home. So it just depends on what the child learns. Poverty impacts language because when you're in a poverty situation, you are also socially isolated. You're in the projects or the hood, where Ebonics is spoken all the time. As you move up toward the foothills in Oakland and all over the United States, you are expected to know and use Standard English, and in some cases you're expected to just completely eliminate, destroy, and never speak Ebonics. For example, many middle-class parents will say, "Don't speak that way in the home, because we're movin' on up." Ebonics is not allowed, or is at least discouraged.

Her analysis of the impact of social class illustrates the complex relationship between social class and language acquisition and highlights that social isolation brought on by poverty can also be a significant barrier to acquiring language skills. Another teacher commented about her thinking about Ebonics and social class:

> Income impacts language just like being black impacts language. Some children are raised being monolingual, others are raised bilingually. For example, I learned English in the home because my mother, who's now 80, learned English. My grandmother, however, didn't learn English. She could read a little bit, but she didn't learn English. My grandmother only used Ebonics for 94 years without really needing or knowing Standard English. The point I'm making is that our children, in many cases, only speak Ebonics in the home and only hear Ebonics in the home because their parents don't know anything else and they haven't been taught anything else.

While it appears quite clear that social class was a major factor relevant to learning Standard English, the Ebonics resolution and subsequent policy recommendations made virtually no mention of the influence of social class. The focus on ethnicity, while important, did not confront the fact that Ebonics is a product of both African language systems as well as social isolation due to poverty. As with the case of the McClymonds Afrocentric transformation project, the Ebonics strategy was not based on a more complete picture of ethnic and racial identity as social class shapes them.

Middle-Class Framing of Community Issues

Black middle-class members of BUFFER were strategically poised to leverage their influence to encourage the board to adopt their plan to transform McClymonds. When Joe Coto left the superintendent post in late 1989, it took nearly a year to find his replacement. When Pete Mesa was finally appointed to the post, he was confronted with an 8.2 million-dollar budget deficit within the district. The district's budget shortfall came along with California's recession when hundreds of companies downsized their businesses and laid off thousands of workers. While Mesa was new to the district, he was well aware of the problems Oakland schools faced. Low attendance, high dropout rates, and low academic testing all contributed to Mesa's commitment not to cut money from programs that would directly impact students. Confronted with the task of balancing the budget, Mesa considered closing several low-attendance schools and redirecting students to other schools nearby. This plan was met with community uproar and contempt largely because many community residents had little faith that the district would provide equitable education for their children. Coupled with financial budget cuts and community contempt, the school district administration had been cast by the local media as incapable, irresponsible, and overpaid (Collier, 1992).

By the time school officials began discussing the closure of McClymonds, the community had already organized and planned to force the district to keep the school open. Mesa and other school officials had no choice but to respond favorably to community requests to direct more resources to McClymonds because in the past, the district had paid little attention to the ongoing problems at McClymonds. Years of neglect on the part of the district administration had further fueled community distrust of school officials. The budget crisis forced school officials in general, and Pete Mesa in particular, to listen to community concerns largely to avoid being perceived as not responsive to the community. Mesa had already made a number of unpopular cuts within the district's budget, some of which called for the closure of vital student support programs.

The debate over whether to close McClymonds thus became a pivotal point where the district's leadership could regain community confidence while at the same time addressing the ongoing and unresolved problems at the school. One of Mesa's concerns regarding McClymonds was the perceived lack of resources and support from the district. The issue regarding the closure of McClymonds confronted the school board with a dilemma. On one hand, there was pressing need to make budget cuts that would keep the district from fiscal disaster; McClymonds would be one component of the plan to close schools and redirect students. On the other hand, the district's leadership needed to have community support in order to carry out the plan. This dilemma made the district vulnerable to community concerns because the district was in the midst of a fiscal crisis and needed to assuage community grievances. The influence of black middle-class members of BUFFER coupled with the district's seeking community support influenced the school board to redirect resources to McClymonds in order to appear sympathetic to the community's concerns for the school.

By keeping the school open, the school board could address the community's perception about being nonresponsive to the needs of West Oakland students. Thus, while the district made a financial commitment to the project, the district's leadership viewed the move to keep the school open as a political ploy and a last-ditch effort to appear concerned about the school.

The black middle class in the McClymonds project ultimately shaped the plan in a way that overlooked the concerns of working poor blacks.

As a result, the strategy to improve the school obscured the significance of poverty in the reform effort. Black middle-class social capital (professional relationships, expert-based skills, and educational credentials) privileged black middle-class interests over those of the working poor. One of the ways that black middle-class interests mediated the transformation effort was through the skills, knowledge, and expertise that black professionals brought to the initiative. The ability to write professionally, to negotiate, easily navigate complex legal and governmental jargon, and organize and develop sound strategy all comprises skills from middle-class occupations. While the skills and expertise of black middle-class professionals are indeed a vital component of community change efforts, expert-based knowledge must be balanced with the everyday experiences of all community members.

The lesson to be drawn from this study is that scholars and practitioners need more complex models of multicultural reform that account for social class as well as young people's identities. Oversimplified Afrocentric models simply fail to acknowledge the complex ways in which young people experience the world. Some Afrocentric strategies simply assume that providing poor urban youth with African images, pedagogies, curricula, and rituals will presumably result in higher academic performance and a greater appreciation for learning. This assumption misdiagnoses the complex problems found in urban communities; it relies on a static view of culture and racial identity and ignores other factors that help shape youth identities.

Black youth in urban communities confront formidable social problems and are required to navigate their way to adulthood through complex and often oppressive community conditions. These conditions might include unsafe neighborhoods, lack of health care, racist school practices, lack of livable-wage jobs, and few productive after-school opportunities. Their struggle through these conditions plays a significant role in how they identify themselves. Urban reform efforts that connect with black youth identity must acknowledge these factors and explore ways to affirm their multifaceted identities.

The case study also underscores that community members who are closest to a problem often have the most accurate diagnosis. BUFFER's original strategy was to address concrete problems within the school such as lack of adequate science equipment, outdated textbooks, and no college preparation courses, as well as disciplinary policies that disproportionately targeted black students. These issues were central to BUFFER's initial plan because they believed that changes in these areas could facilitate greater academic performance among the students. Furthermore, BUFFER members had documented how issues such as high suspension rates, lack of child care, and safety all contributed to low academic performance in the school. BUFFER had also observed how disconnected the surrounding community had become from the school. By focusing on everyday life issues, such as child care and employment, BUFFER's initial plan acknowledged the complex ways in which social class shaped reform efforts in urban communities. Also, by linking academic performance to quality-of-life issues, students would have been better prepared to confront these everyday challenges. These everyday challenges are the starting point to effective reform because they make connections between students' lives inside and outside school environments.

EIGHT

Lessons Learned: A Vision of Afrocentric Reform for the Hip-Hop Generation

WHILE THE PROJECT DID NOT ACCOMPLISH ITS GOALS, THE EFFORT did provide learning opportunities about what works and what can be improved when working with schools in poor urban communities. The story of McClymonds illustrates that multicultural reform efforts that integrate race, ethnicity, and culture into urban school reform are important, but simply insufficient given the pervasive impact of poverty. The first lesson to be drawn from the effort is that those closest to the problem are often in the best position to solve it. Black middle-class members of BUFFER ultimately shaped the project on their own, allowing very little room for student involvement. In fact, there is scant evidence to indicate that students from McClymonds were included in any of the major decisions about the project. While there might have been surveys of student needs from the school, students were not members of BUFFER and certainly had little decision-making power in how to design and implement the project. BUFFER's initial working-class members, who focused on the tangible day-to-day problems with the school and who tried to engage students in the process, had developed strategies that were more connected to students' experiences in West Oakland. However, their plans were ultimately discarded.

BUFFER's eventual failure to include input from students and working-class members is particularly relevant to how the project ended up constructing a static view of young people's identities. While racial identity was certainly central to students at the school, many students viewed the project as an arrogant attempt to teach them how to be better at being black. The promotion of Egyptian culture throughout the project was celebrated at the expense of young people's unique economic struggles and their own hip-hop culture. Simply stated, their day-to-day struggles and authentic identities were not central in the development of the reform strategy.

The curriculum's disconnect from students' concrete experiences created substantial barriers to designing effective classroom activities. Besides, the African principles of Ma´at were simply difficult to translate into meaningful classroom practices. Although the curriculum training manual indicated that the intent of the curriculum was "guided by the conscious attempt to incorporate and utilize cultural retentions, orientations, and precepts of African American people" (Nobles & Mann, 1994), few teachers actually infused these concepts into their daily classroom activities.

With or without the Afrocentric principles, students did not view the curriculum as relevant or meaningful to their daily lives. While the challenge to make curriculum relevant to students' lives is not unique to this project, the lack of student input about curriculum design and implementation exacerbated the further alienation of students from the project.

There are promising classroom practices that connect students' lives with meaningful curriculum. For example, the Algebra Project, created in Cambridge, Massachusetts, by mathematician and former civil rights activist Bob Moses, uses relevant issues and concepts from students' physical environment to teach algebraic thinking. In urban and rural communities around the country, the project uses familiar activities like walking home from school, riding a bus, paying for groceries, looking for a job, and stories about "making do" as the bases for building math literacy.

Afrocentric reform is currently limited by its static and rather flat model of black youth identity and a refusal to examine the complex social, economic, and political forces that bear on the lives of black urban youth. Therefore, the second lesson to be drawn is that Afrocentric educational reform efforts need to be more explicit about the connections between racial justice and economic justice. This discussion is particularly important because black youth bear the brunt of racist economic policy and juvenile justice practices. For example, African American youth are six times more likely to be incarcerated and receive longer sentences than their white counterparts (Ayman-Nolley & Taira, 2000). Similarly, in 1997 black youth had a larger incarceration rate in California than any other group. In 1999, black children were twice as likely to be poor than their white counterparts, and 1 in 3 black children in California lived in poverty. In 1995, black youth experienced more gun violence than any other group, and in 1998 they were 3 times more likely to experience homicide than all other groups combined (Children Now, 2000a, 2000b). At the root of these serious social problems is racial and economic inequality. While there are forms of Afrocentric curricular and reform efforts that do confront racial and economic inequality, most have an explicit focus on African culture, worldviews, and philosophy that never seem to translate to improved quality of life in schools and communities.

The McClymonds project did seek to bring about racial justice by transforming the school's curriculum to more accurately reflect aspects of African culture of the student population, but in failing to go further and develop students' capacity to confront and transform the serious day-to-day economic challenges they faced, the project as a whole failed. Effective Afrocentric reform must connect to broader community change efforts that link school improvement to issues relevant to urban youth such as employment opportunities, crime, substance abuse, and police brutality. Reform and curricular efforts that focus on racial and economic justice can help students connect classroom learning to relevant issues in their schools and communities. There is growing evidence that greater learning occurs when young people can connect learning with meaningful and relevant communities issues (Carpini, 2000; Yates & Youniss, 1998, 1999; Youniss et al., 2002).

Afrocentric reform's challenge to cultural hegemony is an important first step in urban school improvement, but without an explicit discussion of how sociopolitical realities shape young people's lives, it remains undeveloped. In a democratic society where the educational process should encourage consistent, informed, and active engagement in civic affairs, strong educational cultural development is important but simply not enough.

Some might say that it is unfair to expect that urban schools confront these seemingly massive social problems. After all, schools are about education and should not be overly concerned about managing a social crisis. My response is that failure to do so is, in fact, a more serious problem than the social crisis itself. Such a position signals a retreat from democratic possibilities, fosters hopelessness, and sustains the suffering of thousands of black children. Engagement in the issues is much more powerful than retreating from them. Bold and innovative strategies are required to confront the challenges of urban educational and multicultural reform. One place to start is by listening to black youth, embracing their dynamic culture, and shifting our paradigm from thinking about black youth as victims to understanding them as partners in social change.

TRANSFORMING SCHOOLS AND COMMUNITIES
THROUGH YOUTH ENGAGEMENT

Despite the fact that black youth find themselves navigating formidable economic, educational, and social problems, they are remarkably resilient and often respond to challenges in their schools and communities in surprisingly innovative and unique ways. Starting with the assumption that black youth should be understood in the context of communities rather than the confines of institutions such as schools (Pittman & Fleming, 1991), Afrocentric education can be strengthened by exploring the ways that some black youth are transforming their schools and communities. Armed with a deep understanding of inequality and a passion to achieve social justice, black youth around the country are demanding that they have a voice in decisions that impact their lives. The voices of black youth hold great promise for effective educational reform strategies for the hip-hop generation.

The Institute for Education and Social Policy (2001) documented a growing trend among low-income neighborhoods in 2000 to organize parents, youth, and community members to demand changes in schools and develop innovative strategies for community transformation. In that same year, nearly 200 community groups across the country became deeply involved with efforts to reform local schools through intergenerational partnerships with young people. This innovative grassroots reform strategy challenges traditional top-down approaches in which outside educational experts and policy makers come together to mandate what works best for a given community. The Multicultural Collaborative conducted an in-depth case study of five multiracial youth organizations in South-central Los Angeles that highlighted successful youth-centered organizing activities and leadership development strategies that showed promise for preparing youth to change conditions in their schools and communities (Murashige, 2001). Organizing for educational reform has become an effective strategy largely because it engages students, parents, and community members in issues that matter the most and alters how decisions are made by involving key stakeholders. There is a long history of organizing for educational equality in the United States ranging from the Progressive movement in the 1870s to the Civil Rights movement during the 1960s. Today, our educational crisis requires more than ever that we unleash the capacities of intergenerational coalitions to transform their communities.

Intergenerational organizing, however, requires a shift in how adults view young people, and this shift is particularly challenging for some adults from the civil rights generation who believe that youth should follow, rather than lead, social-change efforts. One place to learn more deeply about how youth organize and engage in decision making is in the burgeoning field of youth development. Most notable is the work of Karen Pittman and Michelle Cahill, who were largely responsible for reshaping the field of youth development. Pittman and Irby (1995) identified three characteristics that are fundamental to positive youth development:

1. Society must have a vision of what it wants for its young people.
2. Youth grow up in communities not programs.

3. Youth development must be focused on the overall context in which development occurs.

By promoting youth assets, scholars reconceptualized policy and practice by placing an emphasis on emotional health, empowerment, and exploration (Zeldin, 2000). Youth development practitioners and researchers have also reframed their most basic assumptions about youth to view them as resources and acknowledge their self-worth, self-awareness, and value to their communities.

This shift in thinking can be extremely useful to Afrocentric reform in urban communities because it challenges stakeholders to rethink how to create more effective programs and policies that provide greater support for youth and broader opportunities for educational development in complex and challenging urban environments. Practitioners and researchers now explore how to achieve greater civic engagement and youth development among black youth. For example, Janie Ward (1995) explored how traditional African traditions, values, and norms translate to contemporary social justice issues among black youth. According to Ward, these African traditions are supported by a long history of struggle against systemic racial and economic oppression that circumscribes black life. The struggle, however, also fosters a sense of hope and new possibilities for equality. Afrocentric educational approaches can more effectively reach black youth if racial identity development is supported by lessons of struggle and resistance.

Given the necessary opportunities, support, and skills, black youth can have a powerful voice in educational policy and community transformation. Shifting the focus of Afrocentric reform efforts toward a greater emphasis on racial and economic justice enables black youth to develop a sociopolitical awareness that can translate to both deeper civic participation and greater educational performance. I suggest five guiding principles to consider as ways to refocus Afrocentric reform toward racial and economic justice:

Students analyze power within social relationships.
> An analysis of power within social relationships encourages youth to examine the root causes of social problems. It also requires that they understand how the misuse of power in institutions creates systems that reproduce multiple forms of inequality. For example, such an analysis might require young people to ask who has the power to influence the quality of their education. Such analysis of power often reveals hidden systems of privilege, thus encouraging critical thinking about racism, sexism, adultism, homophobia, classism, and other forms of oppression.

Students connect ethnic identity development to broader issues of racial and economic justice.

Often, inequality is linked to identity, and, as a result, identity is often the starting point for students to get involved with racial and economic justice issues. Biracial youth, for example, develop a deeper understanding of the complex ways that race impacts how they identify themselves as well as how they are seen by the larger society. Black gay and lesbian youth explore the complexity of racism and homophobia and develop a more inclusive sociopolitical vision for their education. When students experience similar forms of social inequality through a shared identity, they can effectively work together to fight for social change.

Students learn how to promote systemic change.

The focus on systemic change develops the capacity of young people to transform institutional practices that do not meet their needs, and counters the practice of self-blame for their condition. Young people strategize, research, and act to change school policies, legislation, and police protocols that create and sustain inequality. Systemic change focuses on root causes of social problems and makes explicit the complex ways that various forms of oppression work together.

Students act through collective organizing.

Organizing is the process of collective action that attempts to alter or change existing social conditions through noninstitutional means. Often collective action emerges from groups who are impacted by similar problems and share the same social justice vision. Collective action might include the range of strategies involved in organizing and activism including sit-ins, rallies and marches, and boycotts. The premise is that the capacity to change oppressive social conditions lies in collective efforts, not only individual ones.

Adults embrace youth culture.

Youth culture has been effective at communicating messages that promote social justice. Youth culture can be thought of as a set of shared ideas and a common worldview shared by most young people. Young people see the world as a place of possibilities and challenge the adult world to acknowledge its contradictions. Much of the dominant youth culture in urban America can also be described as hip-hop culture. Hip-hop culture is often defined by a style that calls attention to the problems urban youth face on a daily basis through music, dress, and language.

Developing Afrocentric strategies that confront issues of racial and economic justice in schools is not an easy task. For example, reformers need clarity about age-appropriate strategies. Projects that are effective for elementary-school-age students are probably inappropriate for high school students. Clearly, such an effort requires first that young people be given the power, support, and opportunity to be heard concerning educational, community, and social issues that most impact their lives. Fortunately, there are numerous examples of communities that are engaging youth in school and community transformation (Gold, Simon, & Brown, 2002). While the following examples are not Afrocentric reform efforts, they demonstrate how students in similar communities around the country have incorporated racial and economic issues into improving their school and communities.

YOUTH ORGANIZING: THE PROMISE OF NEW REFORM STRATEGIES FOR URBAN SCHOOLS AND COMMUNITIES

Books Not Bars: Youth Force Coalition

Since 1990, youth of color in California have been the targets of conservative legislation that has whittled away educational equity, economic opportunities, and political power. In November 1994 the passage of Proposition 187 denied undocumented immigrants public benefits. In November 1996, Proposition 209 banned affirmative action policies in California's public schools, public universities, and city and county governmental offices. In June 1998, Proposition 227 banned bilingual education in public schools. In March 2000, the juvenile justice crime bill (Proposition 21) allowed courts in California to sentence youth as young as 14 years old as adults and place them in adult prisons. The bill also gives broad powers to courts and police to detain suspected gang members. In response to the growing assault on young people in California, thousands of young people organized the "No on Prop 21" campaign to try to defeat the latest conservative attack on youth of color.

In April 1999, representatives from 20 youth organizations came together to form a coalition of youth to proactively fight for educational reform, environmental justice, after-school programs, and community centers. By forming the Youth Force Coalition, they worked together for a unified campaign that would be stronger by participation from diverse members and organizations. The "No on Prop 21" campaign signaled the first step in a burgeoning youth movement in California. Working with adult allies, the Youth Force Coalition planned direct actions, designed and distributed public education material, held meetings and hosted conferences about their strategy to reduce jails and increase funding to improve their schools. In February 2000, over 700 students walked out of 15 different schools in the San Francisco Bay Area in protest of Prop 21 and demanded that policy makers pay less attention to incarcerating youth and closer attention to better books, improved facilities, and more equitable educational opportunities for working-class youth of color. Similarly, in six different cities in California, hundreds of youth coordinated a strike where, rather than attending school, students held public education rallies on buses and in local parks.

The issues that the youth addressed in this campaign were similar to the issues that BUFFER had risen in their plan to improve McClymonds. The "No on Prop 21" campaign focused on both concrete measurable changes in the school such as better books, improved facilities, and quality of life issues within their communities, such as reduction of juvenile incarceration.

Participating in these forms of collective action provided a rare opportunity for youth to put into practice their knowledge and skills toward issues that matter most to them. The students focused on educational reform issues that hold promise for improving their educational options. The students rallied for greater resources that support prevention rather than incarceration, higher pay for teachers, and increased spending on school infrastructure and materials. Their analysis required that they carefully study California's complex state budget and draw conclusions about how the budget might impact their lives.

Despite the fact that the proposition passed in March 2000, the "No on Prop 21" campaign demonstrated a new commitment and energy among urban youth of color for demanding power in school and community reform efforts. For example, in 2001 the Ella Baker Center for Human Rights in Oakland, California, formed Books Not Bars (BNB), a coalition of youth organizers, educators, and community members dedicated to reallocating public resources from juvenile incarceration to educational opportunities and school improvement initiatives. BNB organizes and educates youth in schools about the ways in which large corporations benefit from public dollars directed at incarcerating large numbers of youth of color. Their goal is to rehabilitate youth and community members who have made mistakes in their lives through education and restorative justice principles. Through partnerships with adult allies, BNB combines public education, grassroots organizing, direct action, and advocacy related to criminal justice policy to reform schools. BNB sees the plight of urban school reform intimately tied to issues of juvenile justice. California's rapid expansion of prisons, jails, and other correctional facilities since the 1990s, coupled with the state's dramatic reduction in per pupil spending, has prompted BNB to seek alternative sentencing practices and promote the redistribution of public dollars to go toward educational issues.

In May 2001, 70 young people from BNB marched into a meeting of the California Board of Corrections in order to convince the board to deny preapproved state funding for Alameda County to build the largest juvenile hall in the country. For about 2 years Alameda County officials had been pushing to build a massive 330-bed juvenile hall and just needed to have it "rubber-stamped" by the full Board of Corrections. Armed with statistics, reports, and financial forecasts, young people persuasively argued to the Board of Corrections a sound rationale that prompted the board to deny funding to Alameda County. In a 10 to 2 vote, the board rejected Alameda County's 2.3-million-dollar funding request to build the prison. While not explicitly focused on educational reform issues, the BNB campaign signaled to educational experts the power and value of youth-led initiatives.

Similarly, in October 2001 youth gathered and formed the "Schools Not Jails" campaign and set up a network of youth activists in California who organize around various educational reform issues. The campaign has three demands: (1) to create educational priority zones in low-income communities of color where schools would get significant funding and resources; (2) to have a statewide review that would assess the effectiveness of standardized testing; and (3) to support a statewide effort to have every school in California offer ethnic studies, women's studies, and gay and lesbian studies for its students (Schools Not Jails, n.d.). Students involved in the "Schools Not Jails" campaign made clear connections between youth incarceration and educational resources. One youth participant commented:

> At my school, the bathrooms have no stalls, no toilet paper, no paper towels, and they stink. Ceiling tiles are falling on people in class because of water leaking from the roof. They say that there is no money to improve our schools but there seems to be enough money to build jails and a police station with carpets, TV, all the hi-tech stuff. (Martinez, 1998)

When youth organize for racial and economic justice, they make connections between the local concrete conditions in their schools and communities and how larger social systems can be transformed to better meet their needs. These strategies can strengthen efforts like Afrocentric reform by engaging youth and developing their capacities for greater civic engagement.

One effective strategy to mobilize youth was the use of hip-hop youth culture. Many involved with organizing for racial and economic justice have used hip-hop culture as an organizing vehicle. For example, while youth organized to defeat Proposition 21 in California, youth organizations, community activists, and local hip-hop artists joined forces and organized hip-hop concerts to conduct mass political education and distributed flyers with youthful graffiti art that encouraged disenfranchised youth to vote and participate in the political process. A well-known Bay Area hip-hop artist and participant in the organizing effort commented:

> Culturally, a lot of young people do not read newspapers or even if you pass them a flyer, they might read it but it's not as real to them because it's an old way of organizing. So hip-hop can bring us new tools to organize people with. (Sydell, 2000, p. 1)

The strategy to design flyers, host hip-hop concerts that politically educate thousands of youth, and distribute hip-hop music with political messages proved to be a powerful organizing strategy.

Youth United for Change

In Philadelphia, youth between the ages of 14–19 comprise 8 percent of the population. Impacted by issues of overcrowding in their schools, safety, decent housing, and lack of after-school activities, high school students formed Youth United for Change (YUC), an organization of youth who fight for educational equity in their schools and communities and work together to hold schools and public officials accountable for services and policies that directly impact their lives.

Since 1994, Youth United for Change has been organizing high school students to improve the quality of their education. For the past 6 years, they have been working closely with school administrators, principals, and teachers to redirect resources toward academic preparation for college. YUC believes that strong public schools build strong communities because when young people are deeply engaged in a democratic process, they are less likely to commit crime. Five years of organizing youth at three local high schools resulted in a platform entitled "Education is a right, not a privilege," which is supported by adult allies from the Eastern Philadelphia Organizing Project, a faith-based organization of 20 congregations, parent associations, and neighborhood institutions representing more than 30,000 families in East Philadelphia. The YUC platform addresses three primary issues related to economic and racial justice.

The first issue in the YUC platform is *transportation*. YUC estimates that Philadelphia students spend on average $9.00 a week on public transportation to get to and from school. For many families who do not have jobs or whose parents cannot afford public transportation, simply attending school becomes a difficult task. YUC points out that cities such as New York and Boston have taken the lead in providing free transportation to school-aged youth on weekdays until 7:00 p.m. Free public transportation would increase attendance and help support youth from families with limited financial means.

The second issue that YUC addresses is *availability of internships and after-school programs.* The relocation of jobs from the urban communities has left many students in East Philadelphia without opportunities to work and gain valuable work experience. YUC believes that internships give high school students a better advantage in the working world by teaching responsibility and broadening their perspective on what careers are available. More after-school opportunities will also keep Philadelphia teens out of trouble. YUC's stance is, since their schools fail to provide them with these valuable opportunities, schools should begin addressing these issues by keeping the building open until 7:00 or 8:00 p.m. so that after-school programs can be more available. In addition to advocating for after-school programs, YUC also encourages directing resources to support schools in purchasing updated books, computers, and availability to the Internet.

The third YUC issue is *safety to and from school and security while in school.* After several incidents of violence inflicted upon students on their way to school, YUC members at one local high school demanded that the mayor, within the first few months of his term, conduct a survey of all the neighborhood high schools and make a public report on how safe and secure they are. YUC members at one of the local high schools worked with representatives from local police, businesses, and city government to improve the conditions near a bridge where most of the crime occurred. YUC was successful at reducing the number of attacks by having the city keep the bridge clean and installing new lighting and working with the police to have the bridge regularly patrolled.

Other issues that YUC addresses include *reduction of class size.* While the average class size of Philadelphia's urban public high schools is 30, the average class size in Philadelphia's suburban school districts is 24. YUC argues that the school district could reduce urban class sizes by moving teachers who work outside the classroom into classroom assignments and having the city assume the cost of noneducational services such as trash collection and use of recreation facilities. YUC also advocates for more college preparatory courses in urban Philadelphia high schools. After applying to 4-year colleges, students realized that their schools only provided a curriculum that prepared them for community college. They were not being accepted into college because they could not take the required college-preparatory courses.

As a result of YUC's efforts to transform Philadelphia urban schools and communities, the organization has an impressive list of accomplishments:

- The number of students prepared for college at Kensington High School has increased, and graduation rates have been raised.
- Under a partnership between YUC and the school, college preparation courses are now available in all Small Learning Communities, and the course offerings at the school have been upgraded to meet the requirements that students need to gain acceptance to college.
- Freshman attendance rates have increased and the average daily attendance for the entire school population has increased from 60.8 percent during the 1997–98 school year compared with 77.7 percent for the current school year.
- Bathrooms are cleaner and water fountains are working at all local high schools.

Similar to BUFFER's initial diagnosis of McClymonds High School, YUC also addressed economic and racial justice issues by focusing on concrete problems within the school as well as quality of life issues within the communities.

Kids First

Kids First is a multiracial organization that creates opportunities for youth in Oakland, California to transform their schools and communities through advocacy, leadership training, and alliance building. The organization supports low-income children and youth by engaging youth in policies that directly impact their lives. In 1995 a group of youth, adults, and community organizations came together to discuss issues that impacted youth in Oakland. Their discussion revealed that young people did not feel safe, respected, or supported, and often get targeted as the "problem." Youth from several local schools in Oakland surveyed over 1,000 of their peers to learn what they thought about reducing issues like violence in their schools. They learned that young people would have a greater sense of safety if there were more places where they could work, learn, and have fun. In 1996 the Kids First coalition drafted an initiative that would require that 2.5 percent of all unrestricted general fund revenues be used to increase children and youth services of the Oakland Fund for Children and Youth.

From March through June 1996, youth and adults formed a citywide grassroots campaign to get the initiative on the November ballot. Two hundred volunteers blanketed local stores, malls, transit stops, and schools to encourage Oakland residents to support the initiative. The campaign wasn't simply "youth friendly," but rather it was driven by the power of youth culture. Using hip-hop and other forms of youth culture, young people in the campaign produced videos, visited neighborhood churches, and circulated thousands of flyers and petitions calling on City Council members to support the initiative. On November 5, 1996, the initiative now called "Measure K" was overwhelmingly approved by over 75 percent of Oakland's voters. Youth working with adult allies had successfully redirected millions of dollars toward educational opportunities and youth programs. The involvement of youth was critical in shaping the outcomes of the initiative because youth provided a perspective based on everyday quality of life issues.

THE POWER OF YOUTH IN PUBLIC POLICY

The foregoing examples offer at least two important lessons for educational reformers. First, engaging youth in addressing issues that most impact their everyday lives leads to more relevant and meaningful programming. These efforts illustrate that, similar to BUFFER's original plan to improve everyday quality of life, issues such as transportation, child care, after-school activities, and smaller class sizes are all central to how youth experience education. Paying closer attention to what students need, and including them in meaningful problem solving, paves the way for more effective school change. Second, in several cases youth culture was the vehicle for organizing, recruiting, and teaching youth about racial and economic justice issues. These organizations used organizing strategies such as hip-hop concerts, flyers with youthful graffiti art, and images of youth themselves, all of which resonated with youth experiences. While these multiracial organizations did not focus exclusively on African American youth issues, they often framed issues in ways that placed racial and ethnic representation issues at the forefront. Youth culture was reflected in the music that was played in youth centers and rallies, the hip-hop graffiti art displayed on external communications, and the language young people used to communicate their issues. Youth from the hip-hop generation are motivated by new organizing strategies that call attention to their struggles, validate their everyday experiences, and provide a sociopolitical vision of racial and economic justice. Youth culture can expand the boundaries of current Afrocentric reform to become more explicit about issues of racial and economic justice while at the same time encouraging Afrocentric reformers to consider a more dynamic view of black youth identity.

HIP-HOP CULTURE AND POSSIBILITIES
FOR AFROCENTRIC REFORM

One of the most significant challenges facing Afrocentric reform is its capacity to connect with, inspire, and move black urban youth toward social transformation. However, many Afrocentric reform efforts, particularly for middle and high school students, are simply out of touch with urban black youth culture and, as a result, experience limited success. The cultural disconnect between the civil rights generation and the hip-hop generation is perhaps the single most important challenge in reaching black youth who are simply not motivated, interested, or inspired by reform efforts in which their urban identities are not represented. While Afrocentric reform attempts to balance culturally biased and often racist curricula by infusing West African principles, they are rarely connected to black youth culture. Consequently, at the same time that Afrocentric reformers address ethnic and racial bias in curricula, they themselves create another cultural bias by marginalizing black youth culture. Without an understanding of and appreciation for black youth culture, Afrocentric reformers address one form of culture mismatch while replacing it with another.

Black youth culture in most urban communities is often defined by hip-hop (Powell, 1991). In my 15 years of training, teaching, and organizing black youth, I have found that hip-hop culture is a highly effective vehicle for engaging black youth in learning. Music, language, style of dress, poetry, and art can all be effective cultural vehicles to educate youth who have not responded to traditional ethnicity-based multicultural curriculum. Increasingly, scholars are learning more about how hip-hop culture can be used as a literacy tool for critical education in classroom settings (Baker, 1993; Morrell, 2002; Morrell & Duncan-Andrade, 2002). Grounded in the idea that students are literate in other ways that are simply not connected to classroom learning in public schools, these theorists explore "new literacy," or nonschool literacy practices that can provide greater connections with classroom learning (New London Group, 1996; Street, 1995).

Hip-hop culture can encourage black youth to change their thinking about community problems and act toward creating a more equitable world. While progressive hip-hop culture functions as the voice of resistance for America's black youth, it also provides a blueprint for the possibilities of social change and has been utilized as a politicizing tool to inform youth about significant social problems (Kelley, 1996; Rose, 1994). Since the mid-1980s, groups such as Public Enemy seized the attention of many urban youth of color because of their ability to boldly criticize and reveal serious contradictions in American democracy. Rap artist such as Chuck D, KRS1, and Arrested Development called for youth to raise their consciousness about American society and become more critical about the conditions of poverty. Hip-hop groups such as Dead Prez, The Coup, and The Roots today provide them with analyses of racism, poverty, sexism, and other forms of oppression. For black youth, hip-hop culture is a vehicle for expressing pain, anger, and the frustration of oppression, which is expressed through rap music, style of dress, language, and poetry. Additionally, hip-hop culture is used to organize, inform, and politicize youth about local and national issues.

For example, in a social studies unit that I have taught to high school students about democracy, I have used hip-hop music as a pedagogical tool to teach black youth about how the U.S. government ensures democratic participation. I would begin with a series of questions such as, What do you think about our government? What is the purpose of our government? What would our society be without a government? What is a democracy and do we live in one? These questions would elicit a number of responses that I would then use to lead a critical discussion about equity and democratic participation. Next I would play a video or CD from either Dead Prez or Talib Kwali, both of whom provide a critical analysis and commentary about social, economic, and political issues. Because the students are often familiar with such artists and have also memorized the lyrics, I use these artists' political commentary as a springboard into a larger discussion about democracy. The lyrics, for example, of Dead Prez, who are often critical of police violence, the expansion of prisons, and repressive foreign policies, provide an opportunity for black youth to think about issues that impact their communities and shape their lives.

By having them compare and contrast political lyrics with excerpts from their textbooks about democracy, they are better able to use their everyday experiences to critique and understand concepts such as democracy, equality, participation, and aristocracy in a way that both validates their experiences and highlights youth culture.

Hip-hop culture provides a number of innovative strategies that can expand and strengthen Afrocentric reform efforts. For those who work extensively with African American youth in urban communities, these strategies might be familiar. These strategies develop black youth ethnic identity through explicit connections with racial and economic justice and through affirming black youth culture. Rather than focusing on how to change black youth and their culture, these strategies use the innovative and creative energy of black youth as a platform to build a strong sociopolitical awareness. There are two promising strategies that would contribute to a more relevant and effective form of Afrocentric curriculum.

Validate and Affirm Black Youth Identity

Start where youth are, not where you want them to be. This is one of the biggest challenges adults face when working with black youth in schools and in after-school programs. Imagine an African-centered teacher who places a high value on African culture as evidenced by the way she dresses and how her classroom is decorated. Now picture a 15-year-old black male student coming into this class with his baggy clothing and his hat turned backwards. The teacher's first impulse might be to correct his "inappropriate" clothing by asking him to wear a belt to class to avoid showing his underwear or to remove his hat when entering a room. While this request might not be entirely inappropriate, it clearly sends a signal to that young person that his cultural orientation is not suitable for a classroom setting and ultimately results in another form of cultural discontinuity between hip-hop culture and adult Afrocentric sensibilities.

Placing a greater emphasis on existing hip-hop culture can strengthen youth's openness to Afrocentric reform efforts because such an emphasis affirms youth culture rather than criticizing or trying to change it. Hip-hop culture emerged from the tremendous economic, social, and cultural pressures black urban youth must learn to navigate. By validating hip-hop culture, their struggle for racial and economic justice is also affirmed. This affirmation is a key starting point for building and strengthening other aspects of black youth identity.

To validate and affirm should not be confused with uncritical acceptance of hip-hop culture. Just as in any cultural environment, hip-hop culture has aspects of both promising and retrograde cultural tendencies. Materialism, misogyny, and violence are often woven throughout various strands of hip-hop culture. However, having youth critique these very tensions in hip-hop culture holds a rich, substantive, and relevant framework for transforming classroom discussions, after-school programming, and the purchase of textbooks and classroom materials.

I have used objectionable material within hip-hop culture to teach black youth a variety of issues ranging from violence to sexism. For example, to explore the concept of sexism, I have shown youth videos by Luke Skywalker, Nelly, Ludacris, and Trick Daddy—all which contain sexually explicit (though not pornographic) images of women. These videos, frequently shown on MTV or Black Entertainment Television (BET), show women barely clothed while the men, who are fully clothed, sit back and watch the women dance or perform for them. After the students watch the video, they are then guided by a series of carefully thought-out questions that encourage them to reflect on the images in the video: "As a male, would you want your sister, mother, or aunt to perform in this video? Why or why not?" "As a female, how are genders portrayed differently in this video?" This activity builds critical thinking skills because the material is relevant and familiar to their experiences.

Similarly, I might have students bring in a song that they believe is violent. As we collectively define violence, individual students are given the opportunity to play their preselected song for the class and explain why they selected it and how it might add or alter the class's existing definition of violence. The point here is that the tensions in hip-hop culture should not be avoided, but rather highlighted, because they make lessons more relevant and interesting. One student commented:

> When I come to this class and have these kinds of activities, it's like you trick us into learning something because it's like we're having fun. Then all of a sudden these questions make me think about stuff in a different way. It's like, man I never thought about it that way before!

Afrocentric curriculum requires that lessons be relevant and meaningful to students' everyday lived experiences. The use of hip-hop and Afrocentric ideas can be effective in developing positive ethnic identity, building cultural awareness, and strengthening critical thinking about ways to improve the quality of everyday life.

Think of Urban Youth Culture as an Asset, Not a Liability

Expanding and strengthening Afrocentric reform through hip-hop culture, however, requires more than simple step-by-step practices and curriculum strategies. More important, it requires a bold and courageous paradigm shift on the part of educators and reformers to conceptualize black youth culture as an asset rather than a liability in educational change efforts. It comes as no surprise that many companies have already figured out the power of hip-hop culture in marketing products and transforming consumption patterns among youth around the world. Though private industry and capitalist greed should not be a model for reforming urban schools, we cannot ignore the ways in which companies like Coca Cola and Nike have embraced the ingenuity and creative force of hip-hop culture. Unlike private companies, however, Afrocentric educators must develop a clear and explicit sociopolitical vision for reforming schools in urban communities. This means that while Afrocentric reform develops ethnic identity among black youth, it should also strive to strengthen the social and political capital among black youth by building strong intergenerational networks of youth and adults who are transforming schools and communities.

Effective Afrocentric reform efforts will require new networks that strengthen relationships between Afrocentric educators, community members, and black youth. These networks, while focused on educational strategies that build ethnic identity and provide culturally consistent learning opportunities, should support youth in community problem solving. This problem solving must begin with developing leadership skills and fostering critical thinking about social and economic patterns that support deeply rooted racist, sexist, classist, and homophobic practices in schools and communities. Afrocentric reform efforts hold great promise for transforming youth, their schools, and their communities once these efforts articulate a clear sociopolitical vision by making explicit connections with racial and economic justice issues.

THE FUTURE OF AFROCENTRIC REFORM

Rethinking Afrocentric educational strategies opens new and exciting possibilities for reaching black students. My experience in working with black youth tells me that the conditions they face on a daily basis need much greater attention on the part of educational reformers. Black youth in urban schools want and deserve a better education, and if we scholars, educators, and policy makers would simply listen to what they have to say, we would learn that they have analytical capacity, creative energy, and the desire to make good things happen in their schools. By including youth in educational policy and connecting Afrocentric reform to broader community change efforts, youth are transformed because they are empowered through decision making about issues that impact their schools and communities and make public institutions more accountable for meeting their needs. Afrocentric reformers should also consider how hip-hop culture could be used as a strategy to inform, politicize, and speak more directly to issues facing black urban youth.

I believe that the greatest challenge facing Afrocentric reformers is to connect to black youth in ways that are meaningful and relevant to their everyday lives. I have seen the incredible power and creative energy of black youth in their struggle for community change. Our challenge as educators and policy makers is to tap into this energy so that it might revive new and more inclusive forms of democratic possibilities.

References

African dreams. (1991, September). *Newsweek*, pp. 42–50.

Akbar, N. (1984). Afrocentric social sciences for human liberation. *Journal of Black Studies, 14*(4), 395–414.

Akbar, N. (1991). *Chains and images of psychological slavery*. Jersey City, NJ: New Mind Productions.

Akinyela, M. (1995). Rethinking Afrocentricity: Foundation of a theory of critical Afrocentricity. In A. Darder (Ed.), *Culture and difference: Critical perspectives on the bicultural experience in the United States*. New York: Bergin and Garvey Press.

Alameda County Social Services. (2000). *Department of children and family services 2000 annual report*. Oakland, CA: Author.

Anyon, J. (1995). Race, social class, and educational reform in an inner-city school. *Teachers College Record, 97*(1), 69–94.

Anyon, J. (1997). *Ghetto schooling: A political economy of urban education reform*. New York: Teachers College Press.

Apple, M. W. (1992). Education, culture and class power: Basil Bernstein and the neo-Marxist sociology of education. *Educational Theory, 42*(2), 127–145.

Asante, M. (1980). *Afrocentricity: Theory of social change*. Buffalo, NY: Amulefi.

Asante, M. (1983). The ideological significance of afrocentricity in intercultural communication. *Journal of Black Studies, 14*(1), 3–19.

Asante, M. (1987). *The Afrocentric idea*. Philadelphia: Temple University Press.

Asante, M. (1996, October). Afrocentric idea. *Emerge, 23*, 34–41.

Association of Bay Area Governments (ABAG). (1996). *1990 census data*. Oakland, CA: ABAG Regional Data Center.

Atkins, C. (1992a, June 26). Budget cuts paint bleak picture for Oakland's poor and minorities: Oakland's school system crippled by future cuts. *California Voice*, p. 1.

Atkins, C. (1992b, January 17). Meeting confirms Oakland unified schools to continue with tough times in '92. *California Voice*, p. 1.

Ayman-Nolley, S., & Taira, L. L. (2000). Obsession with the dark side of adolescence: A decade of psychological studies. *Journal of Youth Studies, 3*(1), 35–48.

Bagwell, B. (1982). *Oakland: The story of a city*. Novato, CA: Presidio Press.

Baker, H. (1993). *Black studies and rap in the academy*. Chicago: University of Chicago Press.

Banks, J. (1993, September). Multicultural education: Development, dimensions, and challenges. *Phi Delta Kappan*, 22–28.

Bazeley, M. (1995, November 27). Teacher strike is looking certain. *Oakland Tribune*, p. A1.

Bazely, M. (1996a, December 22). Ebonics in perspective. *Oakland Tribune*, p. A1.

Bazely, M. (1996b, December 23). A retrospective on school board's Ebonics vote. *Oakland Tribune*, p. A13.

Bazely, M. (1996c, December 22). School board issues clarification. *Oakland Tribune*, p. A1.

Bazely, M. (1996d, February 22). Striking teachers union modifies stance. *Oakland Tribune*, p. A1.

Ben-Jochannon, Y. (1972). *Black man of the Nile*. New York: Alkebu-Lan Books.

Bernal, M. (1987). *Black Athena: The Afroasiatic roots of classical civilization*. New Brunswick, NJ: Rutgers University Press.

Bloom, A. (1987). *The closing of the American mind: How higher education has failed democracy and impoverished the souls of today's students*. New York: Simon and Schuster.

Bourdieu, P. (1977). Cultural reproduction and social reproduction. In J. Karabel & A. H. Halsey (Eds.), *Power and ideology in education* (pp. 487–510). New York: Oxford University Press.

Bowles, S., & Gintis, H. (1976). Education, inequality, and the meritocracy. In *Schooling in capitalist America: Education reform and the contradictions of economic life*, pp. 102–124. New York: Basic Books.

Brand, W. (1996, December 28). Ebonics policy at crossroads. *Oakland Tribune*, p. A1.

Brooks-Gunn, J., Ducan, G. J., Klebanov, P., & Sealand, N. (1993). Do neighborhoods influence child and adolescent development? *American Journal of Sociology*, 99(2), 353–395.

Browder, A. (1992). *Nile valley contributes to civilization*. Washington, DC: Institute of Karmic Guidance.

Brown, W. H. (1970). *Class aspects of residential development and choice in the Oakland black community*. Unpublished doctoral dissertation, University of California, Berkeley.

Butts, J. (1999 October). *Youth violence: Perception versus reality*. Washington DC: Urban Institute.

Carlise, R. (1975). *The roots of black nationalism*. Port Washington, NY: National University Publications: Kennikat Press.

Carmichael, S., & Hamilton, C. (1969). Black power: Its need and substance. In J. M. A. Miller (Ed.), *Black power and student rebellion*. Belmont: Wadsworth.

Carpini, M. X. D. (2000). Gen.Com: Youth, civic engagement, and the new information environment. *Political Communication*, 17(4), 341–349.

Carson, C. (1981). *In struggle: SNCC and the black awakening of the 1960s*. Cambridge, MA: Harvard University Press.

Castells, M. (1997). *The power of identity* (Vol. 2). Malden, MA: Blackwell.

Children Now. (2000a). *California report card 2000*. Oakland: Author.

Children Now. (2000b). *California state of our children 2000*. Oakland: Author.

City of Oakland. (1994). Population and housing trends 1980–1990: A resource document for the Oakland general plan update. In July (Ed.), *Office of Planning and Building Comprehensive Planning Division*. Working Paper #1.

Coalition for West Oakland Revitalization. (1994). West Oakland community: Existing conditions statement. Oakland, CA: Author

Collier, M. (1992, May 24). Poll shows lack of faith in schools. *Oakland Tribune*, p. A16.

Commission for Positive Change in the Oakland Public Schools. (1992). *Keeping children in school: Sounding the alarm on suspensions*. Oakland, CA: Urban Strategies Council.

Connell, R. W. (1994). Poverty and education. *Harvard Educational Review, 64*(2), 125–149.

Cookson, P. W., Sadovnik, A., & Semel, S. (1992). *International handbook of educational reform*. New York: Greenwood Press.

Cotton, P. (1995). *Fourth annual distinguished nommo lectures series: Commemorative program 1995–1996*. Oakland, CA: African-Centered Transformation Project.

Crouchett, L. P., Bunch, L., & Winnacker, M. (1989). *Visions toward tomorrow: The history of the East Bay Afro-American community 1852–1977*. Oakland, CA: Northern California Center for Afro-American History and Life.

Cruse, H. (1967). *The crisis of the Negro intellectual*. New York: William Morrow.

Cunningham, T. (1996, Feb 18). Oakland talks stall. Sides dig in heals. *Oakland Tribune*, p. A5.

Cutler, J. (1991, April 19). Shortfall could close schools, force layoffs. *Oakland Tribune*, p. A1.

Davis, M. (Ed.). (1996). *Fortress LA*. London: Routledge.

Dei, G. (1994). Afrocentricity: A cornerstone of pedagogy. *Anthropology and Education Quarterly, 25*(2), 3–28.

Detroit Public Schools. (1992). *The framework for African-centered education*. Detroit, MI: Author.

Diop, C. A. (1974). *The African origin of civilization: Myth or reality* (trans. M. Cook). New York: Lawrence Hill.

Early, G. (1995, July/August). Understanding Afrocentrism: Why blacks dream of a world without whites. *Civilization, 2*(4), 31–39.

Ford, N. A. (1973). *Black studies: Threat-or-challenge*. Port Washington, NY: Kennikat Press.

Frost, J. (1989a, November 23). Latest schools chief candidate backs out. *Oakland Tribune*, p. C3.

Frost, J. (1989b, November 23). Oakland trustees hire superintendent for troubled district. *Oakland Tribune*, p. A15.

Gay, G. (1994). Mirror images on common issues: Parallels between multicultural education and critical pedagogy. In J. Kretovics & E. J. Nussel (Eds.), *Transforming urban education*. Boston: Allyn & Bacon.

Gilmore, T. (1996). *McClymonds African-centered transformation initiative*. Unpublished master's thesis. San Francisco State University, San Francisco.

Gold, E., Simon, E., & Brown, C. (2002). *Successful community organizing for school reform*. Chicago: Cross City Campaign for Urban School Reform.

Grabowicz, P. (1989, August 8). School official indicted on grand theft charge. *Oakland Tribune*, p. A1.

Grabowicz, P., & Frost, J. (1989a, July 26). Oakland schools employees charged in major theft probe. *Oakland Tribune*, p. A1.

Grabowicz, P., & Frost, J. (1989b, July 27). How 6 employees allegedly bilked Oakland schools. *Oakland Tribune*, p. A1.

Grabowicz, P., & Frost, J. (1989c, July 28). Two new cases in Oakland school probe. *Oakland Tribune*, p. A1.

Gushiken, M., Hillmer, J., & Noguera, R. (1988). *The Prescott community plan*. Oakland: The Prescott Community; City of Oakland Office of Community Development.

Guthrie, J. (June, 1985). Schooling in Oakland: The Challenge, Phase I. (Report for the Oakland Unified School District). Berkeley, CA: Strategic Planning Associates, University of California.

Hale-Benson, J. (1986). *Black children: Their roots, culture and learning styles*. Baltimore: Johns Hopkins University Press.

Hall, P. A. (1991). Beyond Afrocentrism: Alternatives for African American studies. *Western Journal of Black Studies, 14*(4), 207–212.

Hare, N. (1969). The case for separatism: "black perspective." In J. McEvoy & A. Miller (Eds.), *Black power and student rebellion* (pp. 233–234). Belmont: Wadsworth.

Harris, H., Grabowicz, P., & Frost, J. (1989, July 15). Accused school foreman denies he stole property. *Oakland Tribune*, p. A1.

Harris, N. (1992). A philosophical basis for an Afrocentric orientation. *Western Journal of Black Studies, 16*(3), 154–159.

Hayes, E. (1972). *Power structure and urban policy: Who rules in Oakland*. New York: McGraw-Hill.

Haymes, S. (1995a). *Race, culture, and the city: A pedagogy for black urban struggle*. Albany: State University of New York Press.

Haymes, S. (1995b). White culture and the politics of racial difference: Implications for multiculturalism. In C. E. Sleeter & P. L. McLaren (Eds.), *Multicultural education, critical pedagogy and the politics of difference*. Albany: State University of New York Press.

Henderson, E. A. (1995). *Afrocentrism and world politics: Towards a new paradigm*. Westport, CT: Praeger.

Hilliard, A. G. (Ed.). (1978). *Free your mind, return to the source: The African origin of civilization*. San Francisco: Urban Institute for Human Services.

Hilliard, A. G., Payton-Stewart, L., & Obadele Williams, L. (1990). *Infusion of African and African American content in the school curriculum: Proceedings of the first national conference, October 1989*. Morriston, NJ: Aaron Press.

Hilliard, D., & Weise, D. (2002). *The Huey P. Newton reader*. New York: Seven Stories Press.

Hine, D. C. (1992). The black studies movement: Afrocentric-traditionalist-feminist paradigms for the next stage. *The Black Scholar, 22*(3), 11–18.

Hochschild, J. L. (1995). *Facing up to the American dream: Race, class and the soul of the nation*. Princeton, NJ: Princeton University Press.

Horwitz, S. (1995, September). D.C. schools open another chapter on Afrocentrisim. *The Washington Post*, p. B1.

Howe, S. (1998). *Afrocentrism: Mythical pasts and imagined homes*. London: Verso.

Hytha, M. (1985, June 25). Report flunks Oakland public schools. *The Montclarion*, p. 2.

Institute for Education and Social Policy. (2001). *Mapping the field of organizing for school improvement*. New York: California Tomorrow; Southern Echo.

Jackson, C. (1991, March 15). Oakland Afrocentric project is hope for young, black males, SF State black studies professor believes. *California Voice*, p. 3.

Jackson, J. G. (1939). *Ethiopia and the origin of civilization*. Baltimore: Black Classic Press.

Jones, R. L. (Ed.). (1991). *African philosophy: Foundation for black psychology*. Berkeley: Cobb & Henry.

Karenga, M. (1989). *Introduction to black studies*. Los Angeles: Sankore Press.

Karp, S. (1991, June). Is all black all male all right? *Z Magazine*, 87–91.

Kelley, R. (1996). Kickn' reality, kickn' ballistics: Gangsta rap and postindustrial Los Angeles. In W. E. Perkins (Ed.), *Droppin' science: Critical essays on rap music and hip-hop culture*. Philadelphia: Temple University Press.

Kershaw, T. (1992). Afrocentrism and the Afrocentric method. *Western Journal of Black Studies, 16*(3), 160–168.

Kitwana, B. (2002). *The hip-hop generation: Young black and the crisis in African American culture* (1st ed.). New York: Basis Civitas Books.

Klotz, I. M. (1993). Multicultural perspectives in science education: One prescription for failure. *Phi Delta Kappan, 75*(3), 266–270.

Kunjufu, J. (1985). *The conspiracy to destroy black boys*. Chicago: African American Images.

Ladson-Billings, G. (1992). Liberatory consequences of literacy: A case of culturally relevant instruction for African American students. *Journal of Negro Education, 61*(3), 378–391.

Leake, D. (1992). Island of hope: Milwaukee's African American immersion schools. *Journal of Negro Education, 61*(1), 24–29.

Lee, C. (1994). *African-centered pedagogy: Complexities and possibilities*. Trenton, NJ: Africa World Press.

Lefkowitz, M. R. (1993, April 7). Afrocentrists wage war on ancient Greeks. *Wall Street Journal*, p. A14.

Lefkowitz, M. R. (1996). *Not out of Africa: How Afrocentrism became an excuse to teach myth as history*. New York: Basic Books.

Lemelle, S. (1993). The politics of cultural existence: Pan-Africanism, historical materialism and Afrocentricity. *Race and Class, 35*(1), 94–112.

Lemke-Santagelo, G. (1997). Deindustrialization, poverty. Unpublished manuscript. University of California, Berkeley.

Li, D. (1992, December 11). State teacher strike possible. *Oakland Tribune*, p. B3.

MacLeod, J. (1985). *Ain't no makin' it: Aspirations and attainment in a low-income neighborhood*. Boulder, CO: Westview.

Mahoney, B. (1992, May 29). Security an issue for school vote. *Oakland Tribune*, p. A3.

Males, M. (1996). *The scapegoat generation: America's war on adolescents*. Monroe, ME: Common Courage Press.

Males, M. (1999). *Framing youth: Ten myths about the next generation*. Monroe, ME: Common Courage Press.

Males, M., & Macallair, D. (2000). *The color of justice*. Washington, DC: Building Blocks for Youth.

Marable, M. (1984). *Race, reform and rebellion: The second reconstruction in black America, 1945–1982*. Jackson: University of Mississippi Press.

Marable, M. (1992). Blueprint for black studies and multiculturalism. *The Black Scholar, 22*(3), 32.

Marable, M. (1993). Beyond racial identity politics: Towards a liberation theory for multicultural democracy. *Race and Class, 35*(1), 113–130.

Marable, M. (1996). Toward a Pan-African manifesto for the twenty-first century. In *Speaking truth to power* (pp. 206–212). Boulder, CO: Westview Press.

Marable, M., & Lullings, L. (1994). The divided mind of black America: Race, ideology and politics in the post civil rights era. *Race & Class, 36*(1), 61–72.

Martinez, E. (1998). High school students in the lead: Massive walkouts in California have important lessons for all organizers. *Z Magazine, 11*(6), 41–45.

May, J. (1973). *Struggle for authority: A comparison of four social change programs in Oakland, California*. Unpublished doctoral dissertation, University of California, Berkeley.

McCarthy, C. (1988). Rethinking liberal and radical perspectives on racial inequality in schooling: Making the case for nonsynchrony. *Harvard Educational Review, 58*(3), 265–279.

McCarthy, C. (1995). The problem with origins: Race and the contrapuntal nature of the educational experience. In C. E. Sleeter & P. L. McLaren (Eds.), *Multicultural education, critical pedagogy, and the politics of difference* (pp. 105–128). Albany: State University of New York Press.

McEvoy, J., & Miller, A. (1969). San Francisco state "On strike, shut it down". In J. McEvoy & A. Miller (Eds.), *Black power and student rebellion* (pp. 12–30). Belmont: Wadsworth.

McLaughlin, M. W. (1993). Casting the self: Frames for identity and dilemmas for policy. In S. B. Heath & M. W. McLaughlin (Eds.), *Identity and inner-city youth: Beyond ethnicity and gender*. New York: Teachers College Press.

Milwaukee Public Schools. (1990). *Educating African American males: A dream deferred*. Milwaukee, WI: African American Male Task Force.

Morrell, E. (2002). Toward a critical pedagogy of popular culture: Literacy development among urban youth. *Journal of Adolescent and Adult Literacy, 46*(1), 72–77.

Morrell, E., & Duncan-Andrade, J. M. R. (2002). Promoting academic literacy with urban youth through engaging hip-hop culture. *English Journal, 91*(6), 88.

Murashige, M. (2001). *The future of change: Youth perspectives on social justice and cross-cultural collaborative action in Los Angeles*. Los Angeles: Multicultural Collaborative.

Murrell, P. (1993). Afrocentric immersion: Academic and personal development of African American males in public schools. In T. Perry & J. W. Fraser (Eds.), *Freedom's plow: Teaching in the multicultural classroom.* New York: Routledge.

Murtadha, K. (1995). An African-centered pedagogy in dialogue with liberatory multiculuralism. In C. E. Sleeter & P. L. McLaren (Eds.), *Multicultural education, critical pedagogy, and the politics of difference* (pp. 105–128). Albany: State University of New York Press.

Myers, L. J. (1988). *Understanding an Afrocentric world view: Introduction to an optimal psychology.* Dubuque, IA: Kendall/Hunt.

New London Group. (1996). A pedagogy of multiliteracies: Designing social futures. *Harvard Educational Review, 66*(1), 60–92.

Newton, H. P. (1973). *Revolutionary suicide.* New York: Writers and Readers Publishing.

Nobles, W. (1992). *The McClymonds international science, culture and technology high school project; the project to make McClymonds High School a school of excellence.* Oakland, CA: The Center for Applied Culture and Educational Achievement.

Nobles, W. (1995). *McClymonds High School international science culture and technology. Proposed graduation requirements and advanced policy. Orientation to McClymonds High School Afrikan centered transformation (for classroom teachers).* Oakland: Center for Applied Culture and Educational Achievement.

Nobles, W. (1996). *The seven cardinal virtues of ma´at and the development of student character.* Oakland: Center for Applied Culture and Educational Achievement.

Nobles, W. W., & Mann, A. (1994). *Achieving educational and cultural excellence for African American students.* San Francisco: Center for Applied Cultural Studies and Educational Achievement.

Noguera, P. A. (1996). Confronting the urban in urban school reform. *Urban Review, 28*(1), 1–19.

Oakland Unified School District (OUSD). (1992). Professional services agreement between Oakland Unified School District and the California State University Foundation.

Oakland Unified School District (OUSD). (1994). *McClymonds High School WASC/CDE self-study 1994.* Oakland: Author.

Oakland Unified School District (OUSD). Department of Research and Evaluation. (1992). *School district information summary 1991–1992.* Oakland, CA: Author.

Oakland Unified School District (OUSD). Department of Research and Evaluation. (1996a). *School district information summary 1992–1996.* Oakland, CA: Author.

Oakland Unified School District (OUSD). Department of Research and Evaluation. (1996b). *School district information summary 1995–1996.* Oakland, CA: Author.

Oakland Unified School District Office of the Superintendent. (1992, March 23). McClymonds High School project. Oakland: Author.

OCCUR. (1990). *Neighborhood profiles: West Oakland.* Oakland: Oakland Citizens Committee for Urban Renewal.

Olszewski, L. (1996, February 23). Tensions running high in Oakland school strikes. *San Francisco Chronicle,* p. A19.

Omi, M., & Winant, H. (1995). *Racial formation in the United States.* New York: Routledge.

Oyebade, B. (1990). African studies and the Afrocentric paradigm: A critique. *Journal of Black Studies, 21*(2), 233–238.

Payton, B. (1989, Novenber 22). Fighting back against crack. *Oakland Tribune,* p. A10.

Payton, B. (1996, December 21). Reaction to resolution is swift, but loud. *Oakland Tribune,* p. A1.

Peeks, Y. (1995). Request for approval of contract: Center for Applied Cultural Studies and Educational Achievement–California State University Foundation. In Oakland Unified School District Board of Education (Ed.), Oakland: September 13 Memorandum.

Perry, T., & Fraser, J. W. (Eds.). (1993). *Freedom's plow: Teaching in the multicultural classroom.* New York: Routledge.

Pittman, K., & Fleming, W. (1991, September). *A new vision: Promoting youth development.* Washington, DC: Center for Youth Development and Policy Research Academy for Educational Development.

Pittman, K., & Irby, M. (1995). *An advocates guide to youth development.* Washington, DC: Academy for Educational Development, Center for Youth Development and Policy Research.

Poe-Yamagata, E., & Jones, M. (2000). *And justice for some.* Washington, DC: National Council on Crime and Delinquency.

Portland Public Schools. (n.d.). *Multiethnic/multicultural education theoretical-philosophical framework* [On-line]. Available: http://www.pps.k12.or.us/depts-c/mc-me/philosophy.php

Posey, M. H. (1969). Toward a more meaningful revolution: Ideology in transition. In J. M. A. Miller (Ed.), *Black power and student rebellion* (pp. 253–276). Belmont: Wadsworth.

Powell, T. (1991). Rap music: An education with a beat from the street. *Journal of Negro Education, 60*(3), 245–259.

Ravitch, D. (1990). Multiculturalism e pluribus plures. *American Scholar, 59,* 337–354.

Rhomberg, C. (1997). *Social movements in a fragmented society: Ethnic, class and racial mobilization in Oakland, California, 1920–1970.* Unpublished doctoral dissertation, University of California, Berkeley.

Rivers, E. (1992). On the responsibility of intellectuals in the age of crack. *Boston Review, 17*(3).

Rodgers, T. J. (1997, March 2). Ebonics: Empty theories and empty promises. *The New York Times,* p. F14.

Rose, T. (1994). *Black noise: Rap music and black culture in contemporary America.* Middletown, CT: Wesleyan University Press.

Schools Not Jails. (n.d.). *Youth unite to campaign for educational justice.* [Online]. http://www.schoolsnotjails.com/article.php?sid=97

Shujaa, M. (1994). *Too much schooling, too little education: A paradox of black life in white society.* Trenton, NJ: Africa World Press.

Singer, A. (1994, December). Reflections on multiculturalism. *Phi Delta Kappan,*
    76(4), 284–288.
Sleeter, C. (1996). *Multicultural education as social activism.* Albany: State Univer-
    sity of New York Press.
Sleeter, C. E., & McLaren, P. L. (Eds.). (1995). *Multicultural education, critical peda-*
    gogy, and the politics of difference. Albany: State University of New York Press.
Street, B. V. (1995). *Literacy in theory and practice.* Cambridge, UK: Cambridge
    University Press.
Sydell, L. (2000). Morning Edition: Hip hop and youth organizing [Radio Broad-
    cast Transcript]: Burrelle's Information Services, Box 7, Livingston,
    NJ 07039.
Task Force on the Education of African American Students. (1996a, December
    18). Policy statement. *Resolution No. 9697-0063.*
Task Force on the Education of African American Students. (1996b). *Task force on*
    the education of African American students: Recommendations. Oakland: Oakland
    Unified School District.
Toch, T. (1991). Afrocentric schools: Fight a racist legacy. *U.S. News and World*
    Report, 111(24), 74–75.
United States. Bureau of Labor Statistics. (1950, June). Postwar status of Negro
    workers in the San Francisco area. *Monthly Labor Review,* 612–615.
United States. Bureau of the Census. (1973, May). *1970 census population: Subject*
    reports Negro population. San Francisco-Oakland: U.S. Department of Com-
    merce; Bureau of the Census.
United States. Bureau of the Census. (1963). *Census of population: 1960: Character-*
    istics of the population, part 6 California. Washington DC: Government Print-
    ing Office.
United States. Bureau of the Census. (2000). Census 2000. SF 1, DP1-DP4.
Urban Strategies Council. (1995). *A chance for every child 2: Propects for Oakland's*
    infants, children and youth in the 1990s and beyond. Oakland, CA: Urban Strate-
    gies Council.
Urban Strategies Council. (1996). *Call to action: An Oakland blueprint for youth de-*
    velopment. Oakland, CA: Author.
Wagner, V. (1996, February 16). Oakland schools strike: Day 2. *San Francisco*
    Examiner, p. A1.
Ward, J. (1995). Cultivating a morality of care in African American adolescents:
    A culture-based model of violence prevention. *Harvard Educational Review,*
    65(2), 1–14.
Warfield, N. (1992). The rites of passage movement: A resurgence of African-
    centered practices for socializing African American youth. *Journal of Negro*
    Education, 61(1), 471–482.
We Interrupt This Message. (2001). *Soundbites and cellblocks: Analysis of the juvenile*
    justice media debate and a case study of California's proposition 21. San Francisco:
    Author.
Welcome to Ebonics II: The backlash. English spoken here, by African Americans.
    (1996). *Oakland Tribune,* p. A1.

Wilkens, R. (1969). The case against separatism: "black Jim Crow." In J. McEvoy & A. Miller (Eds.), *Black power and student rebellion* (pp. 235–236). Belmont: Wadsworth.

Wilkenson, D. M. (1996, July). Afrocentric marketing not just a niche. *Black Enterprise, 26,* 72–77.

Wilson, J. A. (1994). Afrocentric fashions—a trend or are cultural expression here to stay? *Black Collegian, 24,* 23–26.

Wilson, L. J. (1970). *Overall economic development program.* Oakland, CA: City of Oakland.

Wilson, W. J. (1987). *The truly disadvantaged: The inner city, the underclass, and public policy.* Chicago: University of Chicago Press.

Wilson, W. J. (1996). *When work disappears.* New York: Random House.

Yates, M., & Youniss, J. (1998). Community service and political identity development in adolescence. *Journal of Social Issues, 54*(3), 493–512.

Yates, M., & Youniss, J. (Eds.). (1999). *Roots of civic identity: International perspectives on community service and youth activism.* New York: Cambridge University Press.

The year of the black author. (1995, February). *Black Enterprise, 25*(7), 116.

Youniss, J., Bales, S., Christmas-Best, V., Diversi, M., McLaughlin, M. W., & Silbereisen, R. (2002). Youth civic engagement in the twenty-first century. *Journal of Research on Adolescence, 12*(1), 121–148.

Zeldin, S. (2000). Integrating research and practice to understand and strengthen communities for adolescent development: An introduction to the special issue and current issues. *Applied Developmental Science, 4*(1), 2–10.

Index

Academic performance: and challenge of Afrocentric reform, 25–26, 27, 29, 31; and challenges facing black youth, 2; and crisis in Oakland schools, 48, 49, 50, 52, 53, 54, 66, 67; and failure of Afrocentric reform, 108–11, 112, 117–18; and implementing the Afrocentric program, 93, 98, 100, 103, 106, 107; and plans to transform McClymonds High School, 68, 71, 72, 74, 79, 82; and what is not known about Afrocentric reform, 6

ACORN, 46, 60, 64

Adams, Hunter III, 98

Administrators: and crisis in Oakland schools, 49, 50, 52, 54, 62; and failure of Afrocentric reform, 115–16; and implementing the Afrocentric program, 89, 92, 93, 97, 100, 105; and plans to transform McClymonds High School, 72, 73–74, 81. *See also specific person*

AFDC (Aid to Families with Dependent Children), 5, 60, 103

African American Baseline Essays, 26, 27

"African Dreams," 16

African Heritage Studies Association, 13

African Studies Association (ASA), 13

African-centered: definition of, 82

African-centered independent schools, 20–21

Africana/African American studies, 15

Afrocentrism/Afrocentric reform: and academic performance, 6, 25–26, 27, 29, 31; beliefs of, 25–26; challenges facing, 21, 24–34; characteristics of, 82–84, 86–87; definition of, 3, 15, 25; and emergence of multicultural education, 3–5; emergence of, 7, 16; expansion of, 15– 17; failure of, 4, 108–18; future of, 136; gap between theory and practice in, 94, 96–97, 107; and generation gap, 32–33; guiding principles to consider for, 123–25; and hip-hop generation, 119–36; history of, 7, 9–16; implementing, 88–107; limitations of, 2–3, 4, 17, 23, 34, 120; as limited success, 4; Mesa's concerns about, 83– 85; opponents of, 21–23; outcomes and expectations of, 107; and plans to transform McClymonds High School, 74– 87; proponents of, 17, 18–21, 26; questions regarding, 4; as social movement, 16–17; today's, 16–17; in urban schools, 25–27; vision of, 119–36; as way of life, 96; what is, 17–23; what we know about, 5–7; and youth culture as asset, 135–36

After-school programs, 129, 131, 134

Agee, Dorothy Spann–, 65–67, 71

Akbar, Na'im, 18, 20, 98

About the Author

Shawn A. Ginwright is an Assistant Professor of Sociology and Ethnic Studies at Santa Clara University. In 1989, Dr. Ginwright cofounded Leadership Excellence Inc., an innovative youth development agency located in Oakland, California, that trains African American youth to address pressing social and community problems. He received his Ph.D. from the University of California at Berkeley in 1999, while serving as the Executive Director of Leadership Excellence. In 1998, he joined the faculty at Santa Clara University, where he works with youth, parents, schools, and community-based organizations, as well as local, state, and national offices on urban youth related issues. His research examines the ways in which youth in urban communities navigate through the constraints of poverty and struggle in order to create equality and justice in their schools. He has published extensively on issues related to urban youth in journals such as *Social Problems*, *Social Justice*, *Urban Review*, and *New Directions in Youth Development*. He is a highly sought speaker for national and international audiences.